The Golf Pro Has Heart
Teeing Up Unique, Happy Relationship Secrets with Fun Golf Stories

The Golf Pro Has Heart
Teeing Up Unique, Happy Relationship Secrets with Fun Golf Stories

Author
John A. Gehrisch

Editor
Cathy Burnham Martin

John A. Gehrisch
www.GolfProHasHeart.com

with thanks to

www.QTPublishing.com

This title and more are featured at
www.GoodLiving123.com

The Golf Pro Has Heart
Teeing Up Unique, Happy Relationship Secrets with Fun Golf Stories

Copyright © 2017 John A. Gehrisch
Naples, FL

Paperback edition: ISBN 978-1-939220-24-0
eBook edition: ISBN 978-1-939220-23-3

Published and printed in the United States of America.

Library of Congress Control Number:
2016918390

J Merritt & Doris Gehrisch Memorial

Clearly now, it is apparent that I could not see the forest for the trees, as they say. As with most of us, many of the answers to finding true, long-term happiness with a significant other were right before me my whole life. I just presume it was "the norm" and became oblivious to its wonder. Only later, after their death, when I most needed them, did I realize they were still here for me, leaving the path to true happiness. All I had to do was look diligently.

And so, I dedicate this book to my parents, John Merritt Gehrisch and Doris Jean Gehrisch. To the best of my knowledge, they were two people who were respected by everyone who knew them. Most even loved them. They led their lives by setting the examples of honesty, integrity, respect for all deserving, faith in God, and faithfulness to and respect for each other. Those are words that come to mind quickly when I think of them.

I am the luckiest person in the world to have had their example as both a child and as an adult. Through this book, I can now share their secrets and where they led me.

Frankly, I have never quite filled the shoes they left behind, though I have tried most of the time. But honestly, I doubt few people could. So, I try not to be too hard on myself. I am grateful to have had them as parents. I know my kids are grateful for having them as grandparents.

The three generations of men shared the game of golf together, and we could hardly wait for each next day we spent together on the golf course.

Unfortunately, smoking took them both from us way too soon. I wish their great grandchildren could have known them. I guess their examples will have to live on though those who continue on in their honor. I know we will never do them justice, but we try.

I also dedicate this book to my parents because, when I was devastated after the failure of my second marriage, I finally found my much-needed answers to begin my life-changing journey by analyzing what made their relationship truly different from most. I could then pursue it much further from there.

Marriage was pretty much the only thing at which I had ever failed. My parents were happily married, totally in love, totally devoted, and faithful to each other for over 50 years. Naturally, I never thought that I would I would be divorced even once, let alone twice. It caused me to do a lot of soul searching for almost two years after the failure of my second marriage.

I began to study the attributes of my parents' relationship and their personalities. They had common threads between them.

Then I looked at other couples I knew or had known through the years... those in *Happy, Loving, Long-Term Relationships*. I found the same traits. I thought about couples I had heard interviewed because they were celebrating really long lengths of marital love and happiness.

In all these marriages I found certain consistencies. I felt like I found the "Holy Grail of *Happy, Loving, Long-Term Relationships*," and it all started at home with my parents.

I was strongly urged to share my findings through this book so others could benefit also.

I hope you enjoy the read and can gain even a fraction of what I have from the study of these successful relationships.

So, thank you Mom and Dad. I am sorry that you are not here to see this, but I thank you from the bottom of my heart for all you did for me through the years, I appreciate the guidance you provided for the family you are responsible for founding.

Now I want to share your secrets with the world, so together we can make it a better place!

I love you. I miss you. Rest in Peace!

Mom and Dad

Table of Contents

Author's Note: I encourage you to read the book in order and not jump ahead to the JAG Formula, for example. I try to present relationship information in a way that will make absorbable sense, so it is more meaningful to you. The book is divided into two parts. The "Golf Gimmes" are golf stories, and the "Hole Numbers" are relationship-focused chapters. Please read them in order for the maximum benefit.

Fore!

Laughter and being a sneaky jokester remain central to this April Fools' Day baby boy. While that's more than enough to endear John Gehrisch to anyone, he's much deeper and more complex, with compassion ever-present just under the surface.

My husband and I played in his foursome for my first-ever round of 18 holes of golf. John could not have been more patient, giving, and encouraging. Over the years, we've enjoyed sharing travels, celebrations, and the calm quiet of home.

When health challenges found him fighting for his life, immediately followed by his marriage crumbling, he earned our respect even more. John Gehrisch did not mope, grumble, nor bad mouth. He simply picked himself up and turned the page.

Now he has turned his insights and wisdom into a book to help others through their life and relationship jungles. A first-class pro in every way, I knew Gehrisch would drive his message home… long and straight down the fairway. I am pleased to have written his companion book, *The Bimbo Has Brains… and Other Freaky Facts.*

Leave it to him to hit a hole-in-one with his very first book. No wonder even Presidents of the United States have turned to him for advice. I am honored to introduce the author, John A. Gehrisch, and I am even more honored to name him among my dear friends.

Cathy Burnham Martin

About Cathy Burnham Martin

A celebrated author of more than fifteen books, Cathy made her mark as an award-winning broadcast journalist, covering news from Washington, DC to Hollywood, California. Her documentaries and specials brought powerful messages home from events including President Ronald Reagan's Super Power Summit in Moscow and the opening of the Berlin Wall.

A professional member of the National Speakers Association since 1995, this voiceover artist narrates audiobooks, delivers business keynotes, and coaches persuasive speaking through the talent division of SpeakEasy 123. A corporate communications geek and dedicated foodie, Cathy Burnham Martin has been aptly dubbed "The Morale Booster."

Among her non-fiction works are
Of the Same Blood: Your Eurasian Heritage,
A Dangerous Book for Dogs: How to Train Your Humans,
Healthy Thinking Habits,
The Miles-Mannered Man, and the companion book to this one,
The Bimbo Has Brains… and Other Freaky Facts.

She also has written a series of KISS™ Keep It Super Simple cookbooks. All her books and audiobooks appear on the site **www.QTPublishing.com**.

Sharing a passion for travel with her husband, Ron Martin, Cathy is a top reviewer for Trip Advisor. She also writes articles for the **www.GoodLiving123.com** blog

Practice Green

My second marriage had just failed. My heart was in turmoil to say the least. I never expected to be divorced even once, and now I was faced with being single again. I could completely forget having a life-mate altogether and be condemned to a life of loneliness. Or perhaps I could take another chance, with the same result as a possible consequence. Or could I *somehow* discover the secrets that only a few in this world seem to know, but never seem to publicize? I told myself the definition of insanity was repeating the same thing over and over, but expecting a different result. My answer became obvious, so my quest began.

When someone lies on their deathbed, for what do they ask? Their boss? Money? Or their loved ones?

Who does not want ultimate happiness in their life? What will attain that for you? If you had to choose one thing, would it be a happy, loving relationship with a significant other?

No matter if you are in a "heterosexual" or "same sex" relationship, the secrets to success / happiness are basically the same. If I can give you those secrets, would you be interested?

First, I do not tell you the following in an attempt to impress you. Certainly nothing of the kind. I want you to understand what makes me feel that I am qualified to write this book and why you should read it if you are interested in knowing The Secrets to a *Happy, Loving, Long-Term Relationship.*

Part of my background is that I had started a wire company from scratch that 20 years later made enough wire in one year, that if laid end to end, it would have wrapped the world 13 times. It became the largest company of its type in the USA, and perhaps the world.

During that time I endured many trials and tribulations. At times I had to learn new things, because I was treading in unfamiliar waters. I made a lot of mistakes. When I was in trouble, I sought counsel from experts who knew more than I knew or were more experienced than I was in that particular area.

For example, I remember acquiring a product line and some equipment from a New York Stock Exchange Company. It turned out that they had the Profit and Loss numbers muddled up in other product lines they retained, so they could bury certain costs that should have been shown to me. Instead, they kept them hidden. The essence is, it was all deliberately misrepresented to me.

Until that point, my company had been profitable from the first year I started in business. Suddenly, it was hemorrhaging cash. I reached a point where both my accountant and lawyer advised me to file bankruptcy. They believed that my only choice was to reorganize or call it quits all together.

That meant letting my dream and all my hard work die in vain, and it meant letting all my employees and my family down, not to mention letting myself down. I just could not bring myself to give up. I also did not want to let down the bank and vendors that had trusted me.

I needed a plan, and I developed one. Before implementing it, however, I sought the advice of a trusted friend, Paul Sticht. He was Chairman of the Board of R.J. Reynolds and sat on the board of the Chrysler Corporation. Paul helped me refine my plan.

I presented it to the bank, and they backed me. The plan worked, and the ending was a happy one.

After I sold that company, now owned by Warren Buffet, I played on the Mini Tours and Champions Tour. Again, I sought advice from experts on how to approach this, what to expect, how to get better, and many other helpful things.

Why do I tell you these stories? I want you to know that I do not easily accept failure, and I seek answers from experts when I need answers.

I have had two marriages fail. Sadly, marriage is pretty much the only thing at which I have ever failed. Most people who know the circumstances tell me these failures were not my fault.

In fact, the Catholic Church annulled my first marriage. Out of respect for my second wife, with whom I have an amicable relationship, I do not wish to discuss that scenario.

I do want you to know that I struggled to accept the fact that my marriages had failed in the first place. I felt that if I had chosen correctly, they would not have failed.

It takes two to make a relationship successful, and usually, it takes two to let it fail. So, I set out to find out what I had done wrong by learning from the experts who had done it successfully. I did not want to fail again.

Thus began a life changing journey.

Many friends and associates encouraged me to share my discoveries, so that other people might also be helped.

When I was first out of college, I was sent to a Marketing course while I worked for General Electric. I remember thinking, I am being taught marketing by an instructor who has never stepped one foot into the real world of marketing. He had never served one day working for a company doing any real life marketing, yet he was supposed to teach me how to do it in the real world.

That made no sense to me. Why would GE not have me taught by someone from the real world with real experience?

Would you rather have your brain operated on by someone who only studied books, or someone who has actually done it successfully? The answer seems obvious.

So, for this project, I did what has always worked for me in the past. I looked at people who actually have lived in what I now call a *Happy, Loving, Long-Term Relationship*, and then tried to identify their secrets.

I was not interested in scholars nor book teachers. I chose to study real-life people as my examples. I cannot give all the possible answers here, as that would take volumes. Yet, some of my most relevant observations are here. My intention is to help, not hurt. So, for the sake of confidentiality, I have taken the liberty to change many of the names, dates, or places.

Because so many of my golfing experiences have helped shape the man I am today, I sprinkled in some of the more relevant golf stories for entertainment, too.

I hope you enjoy the read. Most importantly, I hope you discover some things that you did not previously know or gain a new, helpful perspective. All of us benefit when we learn to think a little outside the box... or, in this case, outside the golf bag.

Season Begins:

Winter Work and a Spring Secret

After being bitten with the golf bug in Illinois, I was moved to Michigan by my employer, General Electric. I met some local guys and began to play on Saturday morning with them. I think every golfer who spends the winter not being able to play, finds themselves going backwards some in the spring and struggling to get back their game until they have played at least a few weeks.

One trick I learned on my own was to choke down on the golf club two or 3 inches, because I found I had better control and more accurately hit the ball and the sweet spot of the club.

Ironically, I hit the ball almost as far. Probably because I was more consistently centering the ball on the face of the club at impact.

I remember my father asking me one time, how I could hit it so far when I was choked down on the club like that? I didn't really have a good answer at the time. I just knew it worked for me.

In fact, I typically stayed down on the club for at least a month each spring, before slowly moving back up. It's something you might try if you are having trouble hitting your golf shots solidly.

I was improving, but I wanted a major improvement. So, I picked up Jack Nicklaus' book, *"Golf My Way."* This would end up being the majority of my formal training, although I also read many articles.

I particularly wanted to stop my slice (left-to-right curve for a right-hander) that most amateurs have, including me, and especially higher handicappers.

I studied Jack's book and decided to dedicate myself to stop that slice during the winter months.

I did not have much extra money to go to a driving range, even if there had been any that were open in the winter there.

However, I had a garage that I transformed into a personal range. I did not have to buy a net to catch the balls, because I got creative and saved some money. I draped an old blanket over a clothesline hanging from the rafters in the garage.

So that I would not have to chase every ball I hit, I put a roof gutter across the bottom of the blanket. It perfectly caught golf balls after I hit them. I angled it left to right and connected a downspout so the balls would roll into the downspout and back to me.

I had purchased a grass-like mat, one normally used in front of a door to wipe your feet in order to hit the ball off something representative of turf. I also had purchased a Swing O'Matic that had movable pegs on all four sides of the ball.

If I swung from outside-to-in, which is one cause of most slices, I would knock down the outside back peg and the inside front peg, which showed me the error of my swing path. If I did it properly, straight back and through, I would not knock down any pegs.

I spent hours, and I mean hours-upon-hours, practicing in my garage all throughout that winter.

The next year I got my handicap down to an 8. Suddenly, I found myself in the top 12% of golfers in the country. It was a major accomplishment. Most importantly, it marked the beginning of more to come.

Hole #1

The Journey Begins

"Love can't be seen, but rather its warmth is like a summer breeze that can be felt and cherished. But remember, you must open yourself up to the elements, to feel the breeze!"

-- John A. Gehrisch
American Entrepreneur and Tour Golf Professional

My father was a scratch golfer playing slightly below or above par almost every round. We lived in rural Ohio, with very few golf courses close to where we lived. He and his buddies would have to drive almost an hour to play at a golf course each weekend.

Dad decided we should have a golf course in our community. He gathered a core of his friends together, and they put a plan together to get local people to invest.

They found some land, and dad designed the first nine holes. He was in the implement business and loaned tractors and equipment to the golf course to build the greens and the holes.

I remember sitting out there on the tractor with my father. I also recall him forcing me to hand-seed one of the roughs on what was the number four fairway back then. What I then cursed, as a child, evolved into a current fond memory.

Dad's vision was that one day it would be an 18-hole golf course. Fortunately, it happened, and he was able to play it for a number of years before his death.

I'm really surprised at how many people I run into that know of or have played this golf course called Sycamore Springs in Arlington, Ohio. If you ever play it, look for the memorabilia framed piece that I donated. It features his original drawings and the witnessed score card of the first even par round shot on the golf course. That was shot by my father, by the way.

When I was about 14, my father put a golf club in my hands. He had me swinging in the back yard a little. Dad explained the basics of the grip and swing, but I'm afraid that I showed very little interest. I enjoyed basketball, football, baseball, and pretty much any sport other than golf. He gave up for the time being.

When I turned 16, Dad got me a job on that golf course he had designed and built with the help of some other community leaders. He bought me a membership for two years in a row, always hoping that I would become interested. My father had even gone so far as to talk the local pro to take me on as an understudy. Dad thought that I might listen to the pro. He also knew that a pro was likely a better-qualified instructor for me.

Dad so dearly wanted me to become a professional in the game that he loved so much.

I declined their offer. Though I am sure that Dad was deeply disappointed, he never really showed it. He never pushed me either. Actually, he finally gave up when I only played two times each year. I just did not enjoy the game much. I was good at other sports and lousy at golf.

We naturally enjoy things we do well. Human nature makes us enjoy success more than failure, and Lord knows I was failing at golf at the time.

After college, I took my first job with General Electric in Fort Wayne, Indiana. Across the road from my apartment was a par 3 golf course. I played a couple times. In fact, when my father visited me, we would venture across the street and play together.

Still, playing golf was not a very high priority for me. Yet, it was fun to do with my father, and he seemed to enjoy laughing at my many bursts of brilliance. (That's a nice way of saying that I was lucky not to kill someone.) I had very little idea where the ball would actually go compared with my intention.

Those humble beginnings triggered something very special
however. There was still little indication that one day I would
actually realize his dream of becoming a professional, not to
mention walking the same fairways beside golfing greats like
Jack Nichlaus, Gary Player, Ben Crenshaw, Lanny Wadkins,
John Cook, and many more. Further, I have become close
personal friends with golf legends like Billy Casper, Butch Baird,
Bill Johnston, Shelley Hamlin, Ann-Marie Palli, and others.

Jack Nichlaus and John Gehrisch, in Nichlaus' office

Lanny Wadkins and John Gehrisch, Augusta 2004

Unfortunately, my father died and never got to see that. I can only hope that he was watching down on me from heaven and got a fraction of the pleasure that I did, thanks to him introducing me to this wonderful game.

Following my work in Fort Wayne, I was transferred to Danville, Illinois, where I became friends with a co-worker, Phil Porter. We are still great friends to this day, which is a perfect example of how golf can forge lasting friendships.

Phil really is responsible for inspiring my love of golf, because he talked me into playing in the General Electric 9-hole league. I was horrible, but I improved slowly. Let's face it. I had nowhere to go but up. I had a registered handicap because of the league, and Phil talked me into playing in a few tournaments the year I lived in Danville, before being transferred again.

My competitive juices flowed. I concentrated, tried harder, and actually won first place net in a couple tournaments. Once I had received some trophies, I started to get hooked on the game.

Phil was transferred to Chicago, and I was transferred to Detroit. When he would come to Detroit, occasionally, we played golf together.

One story Phil loves to tell is about a time that we were playing in Michigan. He was trying to hit his ball into a fairway carved between trees on both the left and the right. His ball curved, as usual, left to right and ended in the trees.

I said, "Phil, can I just show you something?" He agreed, so I continued.

"Set up to the ball as though you are going to drive the ball as you just did but don't actually hit it."

He did as I asked. I then held a club parallel across his hips and shoulders, demonstrating that he was aiming left of his target. This actually causes a golfer to cut across the ball when swinging.

Phil looked at where he was aiming and was amazed. He asked me when I had first noticed this.

I told him, "I saw it the first time we played together!" That was about three years earlier.

He said, "For crying out loud, why did you not tell me this <u>before</u>?"

I replied, "You didn't ask. Now, I just could not keep my mouth shut anymore."

We both laughed, and we have laughed many times since. Quite honestly, I had not felt qualified to give advice to him prior to that. After all, *he* had played much more than I at that point.

To this day, over 30 years later, Phil lays a club across his hips when he addresses the ball. If you are slicing he ball, you might want to try it, too.

When you take your stance to hit the ball, your feet, hips, and shoulders should be parallel to the alignment of the ball and club to your target and your swing path. Think of railroad tracks down the fairway arriving at your target.

The outer track parallels your club face and extends directly to the target in the distance. The closest track parallels your shoulders, hips, and feet, and extends just left of the target.

As I think back on the beginning of my relationship with the game of golf, I realize how much learning and experience I had ahead of me.

Recently, while beginning my personal journey of discovery, searching for a perfect mate, I found fascinating similarities.

As much as I *thought* I knew about relationships, and probably as much as most of us think we know about relationships, there's an awful lot of learning and experience that lies ahead.

I set out with the goal to find my travel companion, my confidant, my lover, my best friend, and a wife who is romantic, affectionate, trustworthy at all times, honest, passionate, good natured, likes to laugh and have fun, and looks at the positive things in life.

However, I did not want to make the same mistakes and have it lead to another divorce. I questioned everything that may have led to my previous choices that had negative outcomes.

With the same determination I employed to study and learn how not to slice a golf ball, I set out on my path to study and learn how to be sure I did not repeat past mistakes in my relationship.

My discoveries amazed me, and they may be just as revealing to you. So, I now endeavor to present my learning adventure to you, so it can be as meaningful to you as it has been for me. For me, this has actually been life altering.

Really, all my life, all I ever wanted was to meet someone who, together with me, could build the kind of relationship my parents had. They were married for six months shy of 50 years before my mother passed away from cancer caused by smoking.

Both of my parents smoked, and I lost them way too young. Through the years I tried to convince them not to smoke, but they had smoked for so many years, they were hooked and chose not to stop. My father finally quit after he watched my mother die, but it was too little, too late for him.

Otherwise, my parents were two of the most wonderful people I have ever known. They were honest, thoughtful, and totally and unconditionally devoted to each other.

I never saw them argue or put the other down. They could discuss anything and respected each other's points of view and desires. To my knowledge, they never cheated on each other or gave the other a reason to mistrust or ever be jealous.

My folks were well-liked and respected by everyone they came in contact with in life. Growing up I was even given respect, simply because I was their child. It was mine to lose, rather than earn like most kids need to do.

To this day, respect is the one thing that I expect. I try to do nothing to lose it, and I expect it because it is all I have ever known.

My parents are the two people I have tried to model much of my own life after, and, as I said, they shared the kind of relationship that I have always sought.

One thing rather amazing about their story is that my father was engaged to be married to another women before he met my mother. He was walking with a friend one day in Findlay, Ohio, when he looked across the street. He saw my mother walking on the other side and stopped in his tracks. Unable to take his eyes off her, he remarked to his friend, "There goes my future wife!"

His friend shot back, "But you are already engaged!"

Dad shook his head and repeated in all seriousness, "*There* goes my future wife!"

He broke off his engagement to the girl he was engaged to marry. He then found out who my mother was, discovering that the wife of one of his friends knew her and arranged for an introduction.

The rest is history. They began a 50-plus-year magnificent love story. Oh yes, and me! LOL!

Doris Gehrisch, John's mother

Long after they'd been married, my father and mother attended his 50th class reunion. To Dad's surprise his previous fiancée had become an author and had written an article about small town living. She told the story to their classmates, and everyone enjoyed it, especially since most still lived in small-town USA.

After her presentation, Dad greeted her and congratulated her. He told her that he would love for her to send him a copy, which she promptly promised to do. They caught up briefly before other classmates stole her away.

Later, as everyone was leaving, he spotted her on the way out. As he drew close, he said, "Please do not forget to send me that copy you promised."

She looked at him and replied, "Merritt, you will receive it soon. It is not *me* who does not keep their *word*!"

WOW!!! Imagine, after almost 50 years she had not totally forgiven him for breaking off their engagement.

From my perspective, he had done the honorable thing. He broke it off *before* pursuing his new love interest.

That is not to say that my Dad was a perfect person.

In fact, I recall annoyance when I watched my mother wait on my father hand and foot. I actually felt that my father took advantage of her.

Finally, I could not keep my mouth shut anymore. One day, when I was visiting, I was sitting in the kitchen talking with my mother, who was doing dishes. My father was in the family room watching TV, after cooking steaks for us for dinner.

He called to Mom, asking her to go get something from the bedroom for him. She pulled her hands from the dish water, dried them off on a towel, walked into the bedroom, and brought his requested item back to him in the family room. She then returned to her sink of dishwater and dirty dishes.

I could not keep my tongue quiet any longer. I said to my mother, "Why do you let him use you like that?" I thought to myself, "Why don't you tell him to get off his ass and get it himself?"

To my surprise, my mother spun and looked at me with fiercely firm eyes that I had never before seen. She said, "Do you think I would take care of him, if I did not *want* to?"

I began to think about all the things my father did for my mother, too. In fact, he had just cooked steaks for us, hadn't he?

He was the mechanic of the house and the keeper of the lawn and a major provider for the family. I also thought about how he would grab my mother's hand and pull her towards him and give her a kiss when she would bring him things.

I suddenly realized that they had found a formula of responsibilities that worked for them.

I began to think about the couples I have met in my life and the ones we have seen interviewed on TV… those who have been married for what sounded like 100 years. I started to realize that they all shared similar traits.

One thing is they always give credit to the other person.

Have you noticed? They don't take the credit themselves. They talk about what the other does for them. They all have similar things in common.

For another thing, I realized that they were both *givers*!! And not *takers*!!

Please do not skip ahead as I have laid this book out to have things fall in place for you better. Later, I will share a formula for items needed for a *Happy, Loving, Long-Term Relationship*. It's all based on the common traits that I observed in my parents and all these other highly successful couples.

So, that is what I know. We all should seek to be happy, and now I have the success formula to both follow and share with you.

 Golf Gimme 1:

City Champ... Just One Shot Away

One Saturday, while I was living in Michigan, two guys in our standing foursome were not going to play. So, last minute, one of my friends and I decided to go out to Fox Hills Country Club and see if we could get on to play, as we did not have a reservation anywhere.

Upon arrival, we were told they were having a golf tournament that day and the next. We were disappointed because we really wanted to play. Somebody asked us if we lived in one of five cities, and we did.

They asked, "Why don't you play in the tournament?" Of course, we said that we hadn't even been aware of the tournament.

They then explained, "This is the City Championship for those five cities. It's a two-day gross tournament to determine the winner."

My friend and I looked at each other. We didn't feel that we belonged in this city championship, but we wanted to play golf. Well, we decided to sign-up just so we could play.

At the end of the first day, I was shocked to find myself tied for first place!

The next day I was paired with the other leader. We went head-to-head for 15 holes, never having more than a one-stroke difference between us.

Going into 16 we were tied. My opponent hit his ball into a sand bunker beside the green. I went over and looked at his lie. His ball was almost buried, and the pin was tight on that side of the green. I remember thinking his best score would be bogey and possibly double. With only two holes left to play, I calculated that I would likely walk off one or two strokes better than him.

Being City Champion was literally within my grasp. That had been beyond my wildest imagination a mere four hours earlier. For some reason, in tournaments, I have always been able to reach down, concentrate, and do better than in the normal rounds.

He took his stance over the ball. I watched in anticipation, thinking he would be lucky to even get it out of the bunker on the first shot. Surely, if he did somehow, he would be long and over the green because there was not enough room to stop the ball with no spin coming out of the buried lie.

He opened up the club face like a normal bunker shot, pulled the club back and cut across the ball which really was the wrong way to play that kind of lie.

I knew the most consistent play was to do the opposite of a normal bunker shot. You close the club face down and hit through knowing the ball will run, but at least you can get out. Somehow he bladed the ball and it did come out which was lucky in itself. It was now screaming across the green about four feet off the ground.

My instinct told me he would be 40 to 60 yards past the green when the ball ended its journey.

And then the impossible happened! He hit the flagstick dead center. The stick made a loud noise as it stopped the ball in its flight. The give of the stick moving backward absorbed much of its impact dropping the ball softly a few feet away.

Then to make things even worse, the ball's spin spun it towards the cup. A couple seconds later the green only had my ball marker laying on it.

That stupid ball went into the cup for birdie!! I saw my one- or two-stroke lead change to a one-stroke deficit, and I was not able to overcome it on the next two holes, losing the City Championship by one stroke!

Honestly, I had no business being the City Champion with an 8-handicap anyways. That was the only solace I could take away from the day, other than the fact I was told I had qualified for the Michigan State Championship. Can you imagine it all came about because last-minute we decided to play golf and had no tee time anywhere?

A few weeks later I made the trip to Muskegon, Michigan to play in the State Championship. As I had never played it before, I went a day early to play the golf course, so I would have some familiarity.

It was an extremely tight golf course cutout of a Pine Forest with out of bounds or a creek running down one side or both sides on every fairway.

Any wayward shot would typically produce at least a one- or two-shot penalty. It was not an extremely long golf course, and in those days I hit the ball pretty far, so I decided to play the course smart the next day and use my 2 iron off the tee for placement.

The next morning I teed it up, with a lot of nerves flowing. I had never before played in anything of this caliber. Hole after hole I struck my two iron poorly, leaving myself at much longer distances to the green than I planned. I was not scoring well at all. I certainly was not playing like the number 2 player in my city should be representing. That only added more pressure to my day and play.

Finally, with only five holes left I decided to start hitting my driver, in which I always had a lot of confidence. Of course, I split every fairway going in, realizing I should have stayed with the game I knew, even if my plan on paper was smarter.

When I got in, I had posted an embarrassing score. Something like 84.

The City Champion walked by and ask me how I had played. I was humiliated and said I played horribly.

I asked him, "What did you shoot?"

He whispered under his breath so only I could hear. "90!"

I responded, "Damn!! I played good!!"

We both laughed. We both knew the golf course had won that day. The one Takeaway I had, was that the state champion shot a below par round, telling me that really good and solid players could score well on almost any golf course.

I knew I had a lot of work to do.

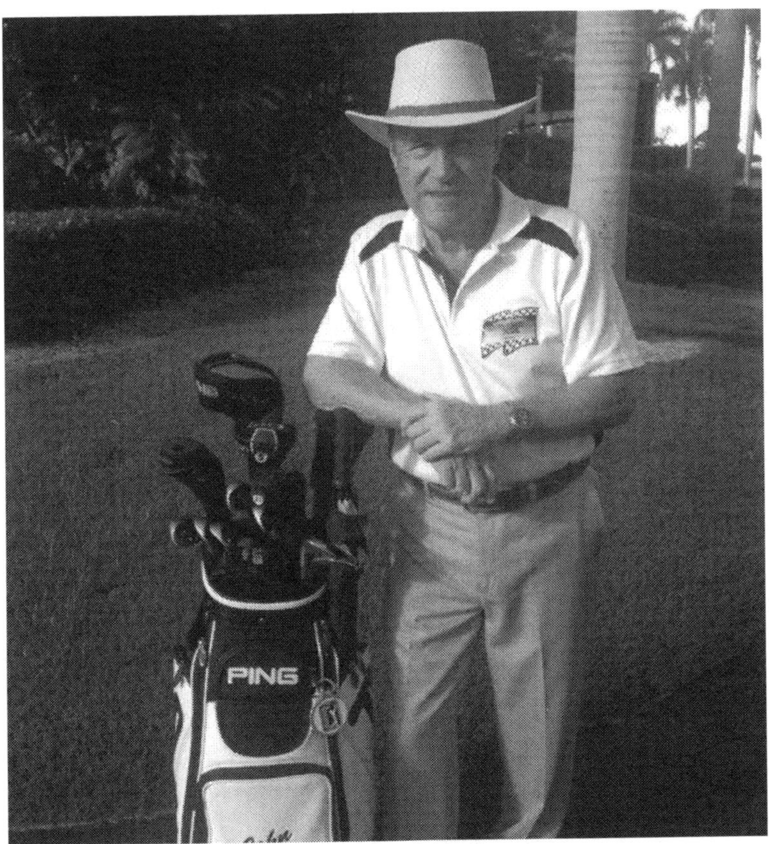

John A. Gehrisch

Hole #2

Help for Tin Cup

The 1996 movie, "Tin Cup," tells the story of a golf prodigy with some serious relationship challenges. Some time back I had the occasion to counsel a friend. As I change names for confidentiality's sake, I will refer to him as Tin Cup (or TC for short).

TC was totally distraught. Following his recent divorce, he discovered that his wife had cheated on him far more often than he had initially realized. He seriously needed to talk things out, so I was glad to be his sounding board. The more I asked him questions and heard his story, the more my heart went out to him.

I asked TC to sit down and start at the beginning.

He began, "I met my wife by chance some 18 years ago. We had almost immediate chemistry, especially physically."

I said, "Did you live together before marriage?"

"Yes. We decided to move in together within a few months."

I asked, "How was the relationship when you began to live together 24/7?"

"It was rocky at times and good at other times," he answered.

"What sort of things made it good?" I inquired.

"Well," he paused. "Sex was great, and I was very attracted to her physically. God, how I loved to kiss her." He added, "She did many things she knew I loved. We really enjoyed each other's company when we were not arguing. We traveled quite a bit, which she especially loved. I mean, when it was good, it was really pretty darn good."

"Using your own words, TC," I further asked, "What made it rocky?"

"Well, a lot of things." He began to open up to me, and I was pleased. "We argued more than I liked for one. She knew I hated to argue. I had previously had a relationship with a woman for 12 years, and we never argued one time in 12 years. Not once!"

He smiled. "It wasn't that we did not disagree occasionally. However, we did sing off the same sheet of music most of the time. It was more that we respected each other and could discuss anything calmly. It was a very calm time in my life… probably the most calm. My wife knew it."

"Was she afraid you would go back to your old girlfriend if the two of you fought?" I asked.

"Exactly!"

"Could you sense if she was confident or not in your relationship with her?" I questioned.

"I am certain she was not, even though I told her repeatedly it was over and I would not go back to my former girlfriend," he answered. "But when we fought, she constantly said to me that I could always go back to my ex! Believe it or not, 16 years later, when the divorce was final with my wife, she told me I could now go back to my ex!!"

Strange, I thought.

He continued, "But also, especially after we got married, things changed almost like someone turned off a switch somewhere. She stopped doing all the things she did to win my heart before marriage!"

I explained to him why I believed that was. I will go into depth on this later, but I do want to add a quick note here.

Usually, men are the ones who change after marriage, but some women do it also.

I further inquired, "I am curious TC. Why did you *not* marry the *other* girl? You stayed with her a long time."

"Sometimes I wonder. I cannot help but wonder if I made a mistake," he said as he looked off into the distance. "She was wonderful to me and my kids from my first marriage from back when I was 19 years old. 100% of the time she was wonderful and giving."

I found that small comment of his to be really "telling!" I will go into more details on that later when talking about successful marriages.

TC continued, "We always had a good time. We had strong feelings for each other. Everyone thought we would marry. We thought that we would marry, too. I just could not bring myself to ask her. I really struggled with that for years. The reasons I really do not want to discuss."

I asked, "Was it a sexual thing, TC?"

He firmly replied, "She would have done anything for me! Out of respect for her, I do not want to discuss it, I told you that. She was the best thing to ever happen to me in my life! When I broke up with her, I lost my girlfriend, my lover, and my best friend all at the same time.

She was having a hard time letting go of me. So, I told her some things that were not true to make myself look bad in her eyes, to help her let go. I did not realize it would make her hate me.

"I regret lying to her. I had never lied to her before. We had total trust, and for good reason. She knew me better than anyone else in the world. I am little surprised that she did not see through my ruse, as she was extremely astute. She was brilliant.

"If she had not been hurting so badly, she probably would have known the things I told her were not true. But my deception worked. She finally let go. I have never had the opportunity to tell her the truth!"

He looked off into the distance again before continuing.

"I wish I could. I am so afraid I scarred her for other men. I never wanted to hurt her. At the time, I did what I had thought was the best thing for her. Now, I truly wonder. She was there for me when my mother died. I could not be there for her when her sister and mother died. I so wanted to be!!!!"

TC's sincerity showed. Even after the 18 years that had passed, I could see that he really cared for her. I could see that he still had a very special place in his heart for her.

I really wish I could have dug deeper regarding this woman in his life. She affected him so deeply in a positive way. But I could tell that this subject was taboo. After all, this was not why he'd sought my help.

"Okay," I said. "Let me ask you, TC, why you decided to marry the girl you argued with if you hated arguing so much?"

He said, "Well, first *she* asked *me* to marry her. I did love her, and I thought maybe if I married her, it would prove to her that I loved her and was committed to her. I figured that perhaps things would smooth out once she realized I was truly with *her*, and I was not going back to my ex-girlfriend.

"But it did not work. In hindsight, I should have seen coming a lot of what followed."

"All right," I continued. "Let me ask you this, TC. When did you first discover your ex-wife's infidelities?"

"Well, looking back, there were many signs, but I had no real proof. One time, she even told me that I wanted sex more than she did. And, if I wanted to get sex someplace else, it was okay as long as I protected myself and always came home to her. She said that she was not a jealous person. However, she also knew I would *never* do that. I don't believe in sex outside the marriage," he added.

"TC, I am not saying that this happened for certain, but many times people give their mate permission to cheat to clear their own conscience for something they already did themselves."

I then asked, "What kind of other signs did you see?"

He paused and then continued. "Many, if I had not been so blind. Looking back our vision is always 20/20, isn't it, John? I had never been cheated on before."

"Can you give me some specifics, TC?"

"Well, one example is that anytime I asked to use her computer for something, she always had a new password. The minute she told me her password, she would change it again. She also kept her phone bills private. In 16 years, I never once saw a single phone bill. I had offered to pay for her phone, but she said that she wanted to keep credit in her name. I don't even know *where* she kept them. I did not look for them, but I never happened upon them either. Now, as I think about it more, I realize that was strange. I was suspicious, but I think jealousy is not good for a relationship."

"You are 100% correct, TC. Jealousy is not good for any relationship," I commented. "Go on."

"Well, she had numerous male friends with whom she stayed in contact all through our marriage. Yet, she rarely talked with any of them when I was around. Heck, I never even knew if she had been with them sexually before or after our marriage.

"She said that just because we got married should not mean that she couldn't keep her male friends from when she was single. So, that is how she justified it to me."

I responded by explaining, "When a man and woman marry, TC, they *need* to change the type of friendships they keep with the opposite sex out of respect for the marriage! You should not have allowed that to continue. A couple needs to realize they are no longer a single person when they marry, but rather, they are now a couple. Everything they do is a reflection on the other person in the relationship and affects that person also. If they cannot accept that, they should not get married. They should remain single!"

TC said, "Looking back, I agree. But I could not make her see that. She would always come back with a statement like, 'I don't mind who *you* talk to TC. *I trust YOU!!' That* was supposed to make me feel guilty for being uncomfortable with her having these mostly private ongoing relationships with men. Looking back, I *should* have nipped it right in the bud!"

"I agree," I said. "But you cannot go back and change anything. So, let's try and get you healthy now! What other things can you point to TC?"

"I told her that if I could do anything over again, I would have spent more time with my parents before they passed. So, I told her that anytime she wanted to visit her parents, even if I could not go with her, I would support her trip. I would take care of everything at home while she was gone and of course pay for her trip.

"The first time she went to visit her parents in Tucson without me, I called her parents' house. Her mother answered. I talked with her briefly and then asked for my wife. Her mother told me that she was in Phoenix. I said, 'Phoenix?? Why?' Well, a male friend of hers was a ball player and was in town for spring training. She had gone to see him, <u>and</u> she was staying in the same hotel." I was stunned. "Didn't she talk to you about doing that first TC, for your approval? In other words were you okay with it?"

"Hah! She never said a word to me!!" He groaned, "Of course, I was *not* okay with it!!"

"What did you do?"

"I immediately called her cell phone and asked what the hell she was doing? She cooed that So-in-So was in town and she'd come to see him. I inquired why on earth she was staying in his hotel overnight and not returning to her parents.

"Naturally, she pooh-poohed it and quipped that she was not staying in the same room, as if that somehow made it all right! I reminded her that I had *not* paid for her to go see some former male friend. I demanded that she get back to her parents' house. She said that she would go in the morning because she did not like to drive at night, and it was going to be dark soon. In truth, she had plenty of time to get home before dark. Besides, she would drive places after dark when she really wanted to do something. She totally disrespected me!"

TC's anger and hurt were extremely apparent!

He continued. "I was supposed to believe her and be okay with it. She had used that night driving excuse before, so I believed it. At the time, it helped me a little. I later found out it was bull crap!"

"Why do say you later found out it was bogus?" I asked.

"Because there are several other similar instances," TC said.

I prodded further. "Like?"

"One time, one of her girlfriends, Angela, came to visit us. Angela had gotten divorced because she had been caught cheating with the builder who was constructing a house for her and her husband.

"Anyway, she told me she was going to take Angela to the Fox Grill later that day while I was working. I had never been to the Fox Grill, but I knew where it was.

"As I was driving home, I happened to see the Fox Grill. Remembering that they were stopping there at some point, I decided to stop in and maybe join them for something to eat. It never occurred to me that my wife would be doing anything inappropriate.

"When I walked in, I first saw Angela. She wasn't with my wife. She was sitting across a table from some man. As I wondered where on earth my wife was, I was suddenly shocked. I completely froze at what I saw. I guess I was in shock, because I truly could not move for about a minute.

"There was my wife sitting not only at another table, but cozily sitting *beside* some man. Seriously. She wasn't sitting across from him. She was right beside him and leaning in very close to him!! As I tried to recover from my shock, I saw him offer a bite of dessert off *his* fork. She accepted willingly. I mean I watched her seductively open her mouth and him fill it with dessert off his fork.

"I walked up and said, 'WHAT THE F@#$% IS GOING ON HERE?!!'

"She announced, 'Oh!! This is my husband" to the man sitting with her. I demanded an explanation as to why this man was feeding her off *his* fork?? I mean, that is one of the most sensual things a man can legally do in a restaurant with a woman!! The man stood up and left us, which was smart on his part. She quickly told Angela that they needed to go.

"I said, 'You have *that* right!'

"I got in my car, still shaking and trying to decide what to do as we drove home in our separate cars. While we drove, she called me and apologized.

"She said, 'You know that I am not into Black men, and nothing was going to happen.' Again she told me that, and I reluctantly bought into it… again. She said that she'd had a little too much to drink and did not use good judgment.

"I asked why on earth she wasn't sitting with Angela? She was supposed to have been there with Angela. She told me Angela wanted some time alone so she could get to know that other man. So, my wife and his friend took another table. She begged me to forgive her. We got past it, and I said I would forgive her, but the image of that moment is burned into my mind. I will never forget it as long as I live."

"Wow!" I said. "Even if her intensions *were* honorable, which I sincerely doubt, I wonder what the man expected was going to happen. Obviously, feeding a woman sitting that close you and facing you delivers all the signs of a woman that is very "into" a man! The parking lot could have gotten ugly for her, once he determined she had played him, if she was."

I continued. "Let me ask you something TC. Have you ever considered the fact that your wife was the one sitting *beside* a man, *not* her friend? Why was *she* sitting close, facing him, and *next* to him if *she* was the one simply killing time so Angela could have some "alone" time. Angela was sitting *across* from the man with whom she was talking. Further, why would Angela put her girlfriend, a married woman, in such a scenario to be sitting alone with another man?"

"Hmmmm," muttered TC. He just stared out the window again, as if the answers to my questions were written in the clouds.

"I guess sometimes we overlook the obvious, because we love someone, and we *want* to believe the best," TC concluded. "And you know, I recall another situation that now makes me realize that she most likely went there *not* to meet Angela, but to meet that *man*. I feel like such a fool!"

"Love can make us blind, TC. Do not get down on yourself," I told him. "It happens to practically everyone at some point for something."

Still looking out the window, TC said, "I'm afraid that my next story will confirm your point of view, John."

I wondered where this was going. I could see the injury my friend had sustained from this woman. I actually think it had aged him. He felt comfort looking away from me, at the moment anyways.

We had met in Scottsdale to have our talk. It was a fall-like day outside. A breeze was flowing down from the mountains, making it feel a little cooler than normal outside. The sky was the typical clear, vibrant blue color, as if you were looking through a pair of Polaroid sunglasses.

Only today there were a few whispers of white clouds added. This was not typical for an area that boasts 300 clear blue sky days out of every 365.

It mattered little, as TC seem to be lost as he gazed out the window, watching those clouds slipping silently past. I gave him a temporary break from my questions, thinking it might be the release that he needed from the strain of it all.

 I let him sit in the emptiness of the environment, void of words from either of us until he seemed ready to continue.

The room was silent with only the sound of a few distant cars passing remotely in the distance going about their daily routines. If you listened intently, through the void came a mystical clanging of a Southwestern Indian wind chime playing its music in the breeze from the neighbor's home.

It was obvious that TC had a lot of pain stored up inside because he remained silent for several minutes. Clearly, TC had felt his heart being ripped from his very soul by the actions of this woman.

It was practically like there were toxins evaporating from his pores that almost anyone could sense.

Making him feel better about what had happened was going to have to be handled delicately. I wondered if I had the answers that could help him go on and be happy again. He had been hurt so deeply by this woman.

TC told me how he was not a big drinker, but he had found alcohol gave him some escape for a few days prior. Men *are* far more likely to turn to alcohol after a divorce. I thought maybe a small diversion might help break up the heaviness in the air.

Finally I said, "TC?"

He mentally came back to the room, as his head moved only slightly from the window.

"What was the final straw… the thing that prompted you to file for divorce?"

Now TC slowly looked back at me.

"John," he began. "I was sitting with my wife at a bar to get something to eat before we went to see a movie. She always wanted to sit at bars to eat. In fact, even when she traveled alone, she would tell me she would still sit at the bar to eat. Her justification was that she did this in order to make friends with the bartender for protection. But she knew I did not approve.

"Further, this is just what a single woman does when looking for a man to hit on her. In retrospect, that is probably exactly *why* she did it. Another of many signs I chose to let her get away with. I mean really, when I was not there, how could I control her?

"Anyway, on this evening, she had asked the bartender to plug in her phone to charge it. He plugged it in directly in front of me. When she looked at the Wine menu, she saw an unfamiliar term.

"This was rare, because she took pride in how knowledgeable she was about wines. More than I was, really.

"She asked me if I knew a wine term. I looked at it and said no. I had never seen it either. I had left my phone in the car, but with her phone was sitting right in front of me, I decided to Google the term.

"When I opened the phone screen, there was a message from a man I did not know. I mentioned that she had a message from *some man*, and she quickly grabbed the phone away me. She then quickly erased 3 text messages, so that I could not read them. I asked her what that was all about. She literally told me, her *husband*, it was none of my business!! Can you imagine, John??"

TC sat in disgust, shaking his now lowered head back and forth. "She went on to say that *she* didn't read *my* emails or texts. I reminded her that I had never given *her* a reason to! Besides, I'd always shared with her all my passwords, so she could look anytime she wanted. And she knew that! She just looked at me and seriously said, 'I never have given *you* reason to either!'

"Are you joking?' I said. Naturally, the very first thing that came to my mind was that incident in the Fox Grill, not to mention what had *just* happened! I could not even believe she said such words to me. Was she delusional?"

TC continued. "John, do you know that she called me the day that she got the final divorce decree and said that she just wanted me to know that she had never cheated on me. And yet, after the divorce was final, people started coming to me and sharing stories. I now know she cheated as far back as about our third year of marriage.

"On one occasion, I was told that she was strutting around arm-in-arm with a guy behind my back, telling people that she and he were going to have children together.

"One person literally saw her in a hotel room. It turns out that she spent two days with a man in the hotel room paid for by ME during one of her trips!!

"The person who saw her said it was obvious she had quickly thrown on a robe, but the man was still in her bed and was apparently naked."

TC went on to explain how she had willfully bragged to the mutual friend, going into some detail about her sexual encounter. She naïvely thought there was no chance it would ever get back to him. Listening to him speak, I tried to understand how anyone could hurt somebody this badly, showing no regard for the possible effect it would have on them if they ever became aware of what happened.

Cheating was bad enough, but how could they brag about it to others, taking the chance it could get back to their mate? How could they do that to someone they supposedly loved?

TC continued, "I later discovered she had also slipped away with two other men during that trip in other parts of the country. The vision replays in my head over and over of her with these men. I cannot stop it. I awaken from nightmares some nights because of it. My heart has been ripped from my chest, John. Just when I think I have possibly moved past it, something will remind me.

"The one thing I used to wrestle with was wanting her to be happy if I died first. Though honestly it was hard for me to think about, I wanted her to know that I had come to peace with her being with another man when I was gone. And now I know she was *already* with *numerous* men.

"Sometimes I feel like I can't take it anymore. I have even considered suicide to stop these visions and nightmares of her with others just to try and get some peace. It's driving me crazy John."

He grew quiet.

"TC," I said. "Do you have thoughts about suicide still?"

"OH!" He said. "I don't think I was ever all that serious about it, but it went through my mind… a lot more than once. I just wanted the constant emptiness to go away, the horrid dreams to stop, the constant imaginations and thoughts of betrayal to stop invading my mind so much, and the resulting depression to leave me. No, I don't think about suicide much anymore."

"Good!" I said. "That is taking the easy way out, TC."

He asked, "Do you mean that you feel it is always wrong to take the easy way out?"

"Well," I responded. "There may be times when finding an easy way makes sense, but *this* is *not* one of them!"

I then asked him softly, "TC, does she know that you are aware of all these episodes of indiscretion?"

"Oh, no!" He continued, "I can't decide if I should tell her that I know or not? What do *you* think I should do?"

I asked, "Is your relationship with her amicable now?"

He said, "Yes, we can talk okay."

I queried, "What do you think would happen if you told her that you know?"

TC said, "She could be uncomfortable. Maybe we could never talk again… at least not easily, like now!"

I said, "Exactly! Other than maybe getting some self-satisfaction from letting her know that you know the truth, what would you gain? *You* are the better person. Besides, would it really change the past TC?"

"No, not really." He hung his head. "I think she would continue her charade and perhaps try to deny it anyway. We would possibly just get into a fight and that would serve no purpose."

He concluded as he gazed at the floor. I knew my next words were critical to this man's future health and happiness.

I said, "TC?" I now paused and waited for his full attention. His head remained lowered.

"TC!!" I repeated louder. He raised his head, and his eyes met mine. "TC, my counsel to you, as your friend, is simple really. Whether you believe in God or not…"

I paused again to assess his attention level. I knew that he believed in God. His wife would not go to church with him and he had drifted through the years. He had previously shared that with me. But I knew he still had faith.

"TC, you do not have to judge your ex-wife! God has taken that responsibility off your shoulders. God does not approve of adultery, as you know. She will have to face her maker one day, and it will be up to Him as to what fate awaits her. Your only responsibilities, really, are to forgive her, become healthy again, move on, and find happiness. TC, she did you a favor!"

"How is that?" he asked abruptly, only beginning to buy in, so far.

"TC, if you had not discovered these things and were still married to her, you would be in the same bad relationship."

"True," he agreed. Then TC followed with one word. "And?"

"And God gives permission to remarry after adultery, TC! You are free to meet a good woman, one who deserves a good man like you. You have another chance to find a true love and devoted mate in life.

"If you can let go, soon you will be spending time with a special woman who will never do to you what your ex has done. You are not locked in any more. You are free to find true happiness. You have a new lease on life. A new beginning TC! Imagine yourself in the future, not in the past.

"Let it go. Forgive her. Only then can you truly be healthy! I do not mean to forgive and allow her back in your life as your spouse. Leopards don't change their spots, TC! She will only do it again, most likely. TC, were either of her parents guilty of infidelity, or did she come from a broken home?"

"YES! Her father cheated, but her parents stayed together!" TC asked me, "How did you know?"

"My studies, TC, my studies!" I repeated. "Parents set an example." I will have more on this in Hole #3 – Parents Set an Example.

TC then said, "One problem is that she is telling friends that I told her that she was just not good enough for me. I *never* said that. I don't know what I could have said to make her even think that. She *knows* why I divorced her."

"TC, when divorce happens, friends almost always chose sides," I reminded him. Usually, they side with whomever they were closer to. Usually, they only hear that side of the story, or they simply chose to believe what they hear from that side. People who do not get *both* sides may not be worth keeping as friends. You will not likely change their view at this point. They will believe your wife in this case. I imagine your *close* friends are *still* your friends. Am I right?"

"Yes," said TC.

I finished the thought by saying, "TC, it is human nature, and you will never change human nature."

"I suppose you are right," TC replied.

"Let it go, TC. Get on with your life."

I followed up with, "Forgive her. No one is perfect, TC. She has goodness in her. You have told me so yourself. She was fair and did not try to take advantage of you during the divorce proceedings. I know that you also went way beyond your obligations to be fair to her in the divorce.

"You also told me there are things that *you* could have done better during your marriage. So, both parties have some ownership in this failure. It is rare for only one person to be guilty in the failure of a relationship.

"Think about where you could have done better, and learn from it. Consider that, in general, you *both* are good people. It just did not work out, TC.

"Never feel you failed in a relationship... *'I tried'* is the most confident thing one can say about a relationship that didn't work out. The love *one* person takes for granted, *others* are praying for!

"Look at it this way. Today is the first day of the rest of your life, as they say!"

Before he left, TC thanked me for being his friend, allowing him to vent, and for my counsel.

As an update, as of this printing, TC stills struggles at times with memories and dreams and the scars on his heart, but he becomes healthier every day. He now has also met a new women in his life. I believe continued growth and increased happiness are in his future.

Golf Gimme 2:

Jim Brown, the Caddy

When I lived in California, I had the opportunity to play La Costa Golf Club a few times. There was a caddy there by the name of Jim Brown.

He reminded me a little bit of Jim Brown, the football player and actor who I had a chance to play in a tournament with one time. He later invited me to his home for a party up in the Hollywood Hills. Football player Jim Brown and I had an inner group contest that day. Every iron I hit, he would hit one less, and he still hit it just as far as I had. He loved it.

Those football legs had a lot of power in them. Distance-wise, he was too much competition for me in my amateur days. Accuracy was a different ball game.

Jim Brown, the Caddy, was not as tall, but he was otherwise very similarly built. He always had a fired-up stogie in his mouth.

He would carry two sets of clubs a minimum of 18 holes a day. Many days he would go around twice.

I have had some great caddies in my life. A few were geniuses at reading greens. Jim Brown, the Caddy, was one of those guys. If he read the putt for you, and you hit on the line he said, it was normally in the cup.

He could assess the speed at which you would typically putt, and adjust the break accordingly. Then, if you hit it right, you were going to make the putt a high percentage of the time.

Jim was also a master motivator. If you had a bad shot, he would say something like, "That's okay. We can find that one, and you can still make Birdie." He never said one negative thing in the entire round to you. If you missed the putt, *he* would take the blame, even though you both knew whose fault it really was.

Jim really wanted to be my caddie on the amateur tour in which I played in California. I elected not to use him because I wanted to save the money. I would have had to pay him for travel time as well as caddy time. I felt that I needed to learn "green reading" myself. Sometimes I wonder what I might have done with him on my bag. I wonder if he saw something in me and my future that he didn't mention. Maybe he wanted to be a part of it. Unfortunately, he was too old to use as my professional Caddy by the time I actually turned pro. Boy, I sure wish I could have used him!

The last time that I played La Costa, Jim was carrying my bag as usual. Somewhere on the backside, we came to my ball lying in the middle of the fairway. I asked him what the distance was and factored in the wind and pin placement. In my mind it was a stock five iron, but I asked Jim what he thought without telling him my thinking. Jim was also *really* good at clubbing a good player.

Almost immediately Jim threw out, "I am thinking it's a five iron, John."

I told him that I agreed, and he handed me my five iron. As he pulled his hand away from the shaft, he said to me, "Let's just knock it in the hole, John!"

Another typical Jim Brown positive comment.

I took my stance over the ball and made a good strike. The ball rose from the ground high into the air dropping softly on the green and taking one bounce before it entered the cup and stayed there!

I heard a scream from behind me and turned around. Jim Brown, the Caddy, was laying on the ground with the strap of two bags and both sets of clubs still on his shoulder. Some of the clubs had started to come out of the top of the bag as he had thrown himself backwards to the earth. He and the bags lay sprawled on the ground.

The stogie was stuck up in the air towards heaven with smoke spiraling upward. He began to thrash his legs and arms as though he was having an epileptic fit.

We all looked at him in shock, laying there acting silly, before we realized it was an act! The whole group broke into laughter.

Then suddenly applause came from the distance. We looked over and there were people standing on their balconies of the adjoining fairway condominiums. They had witnessed the whole thing.

I don't know if they were applauding my shot, or applauding Jim Brown, the Caddy, reacting on the ground.

I have had many shots go into the cup from the fairway through the years, but most I do not remember at all. I know this much. None are as memorable as *that* shot, and I will never forget that one because of Jim Brown, the Caddy!!

Hole #3

Parents Set an Example

"Some people ask the secret of our long marriage. We take time to go to a restaurant two times a week. A little candlelight, dinner, soft music and dancing. She goes Tuesdays; I go Fridays."

-- Henry "Henny" Youngman (1906 – 1998)
American comedian and violinist

If you are fortunate, as I was, you have or had parents who set a positive example as role models for you. If so, we are luckier than many, maybe even most, as not all parents do set the right example, unfortunately.

It is not uncommon for a boy who sees his father hit his mother to do the same in his own marriage. If he sees his father treat his mother with love and respect and vice versa, he learns from an early age that this is the way a marriage should work.

If a girl sees her mother be a stay-at-home wife, or take care of the home and take good care of her father after working a full day's work, she will assume that life will work that way for her also. For years the stay-at-home wife/mother was typical in America, going a few generations back and beyond, excluding war times. The odds of this happening now have changed for recent generations due to financial realities. It is more typical now for both people in a marriage to need to work in order to cover expenses.

There are still countries where it works the way it did generations ago in America. Recently I was in the Ukraine and China for almost 5 months. I found that where Russian- and Asian-influenced countries exist, strong family values are usually still present. This is at least true on the woman's side of the equation.

However, a common complaint there is that men tend to disrespect, cheat on, and even beat women and sometimes the children.

Men pretty much rule everything. Even in a custody battle over children in a divorce, the man is likely to win if he wants them. There are about three women to each man. In some rural areas of the Ukraine it gets as high as seven women to one man.

A girl is taught at an early age by her mother and grandmothers that the basis for a happy home is their responsibility. They are dedicated to it. Most know how and expect to cook, clean, and work outside the home, while taking care of children and their man.

But even there, divorce is growing. Men drink too much most of the time, are not as healthy as in the USA, and often die young, exacerbating the problem for the women. They often have children out of wedlock. Cheating, for men, is almost expected, and many women come to accept it as part of life. It has been this way for generations, stemming back to the war when so few men came back, creating a shortage of men. These patterns have continued to be passed down through the generations.

We are often are a product of the environment in which we are raised as children and young adults. If there is alcohol abuse, drug abuse, or cheating, as examples, it will not be a great shock to see the child proceed through life as an adult with the same mentality.

So, one of the first Secrets to a *Happy, Loving, Long-Term Relationship* is to look at the family of the one you think might be your future mate.

This is not a certain indicator, but it helps you zero in on a possibility or even a probability. Also, please keep this in mind when raising children. Should you decide to have children, you are formulating your children's life foundation mentality.

A single friend of mine explained to me that her children come first, which has caused many men to tell her that they were not interested in dating her. This is not an uncommon challenge. It does present a real problem for divorced single mothers and fathers and people they want to date.

I have seen this stated on peoples' profiles on dating sites a number of times. I admit that my initial reaction was much like the other men my friend mentioned. Then I thought it through.

In every successful marriage, both spouses put each other first, above children, parents, siblings, and friends. Not that I am trying to push the Bible on you, but putting a spouse above all others, including children, is also one of God's laws.

That said, I totally understand why a single parent's kids would come first. I would not expect anything less. Firstly, they are the most concrete, known thing that single parent has had since becoming single. Secondly, these children are a parent's flesh and blood. So, it is normal that they would come first for now.

Any man or woman that does not understand and respect this is not worthy of a single parent's time to even date. However, once a couple makes a mutual commitment to each other, the children must no longer come first. The adult person we select as a partner must come first for you, and you for them, above all other people.

This does not mean you should love your children any less. It does not mean they should not be your second highest priority in life. And if you chose the right partner, they will love your children as though they were their very own, because they are a living part of you.

Your future husband or wife must accept not only you in his life, but another man or woman's children. That is asking a lot, but not if it is the right person for you. As I said, your spouse will see them as an extension of you, the most important person in their life. Together you will raise them as an essential part of the family unit the two of you create together.

The children will also benefit by seeing how a *Happy, Loving, Long-Term Relationship* should work. You both are setting the examples from which the children will learn. Children raised in this sort of environment, statistically, have a far better chance of being happy themselves in marriage and relationships.

Children coming from divorce have a much higher chance of becoming divorced themselves.

It is vitally important for a couple to always back each other in parenting decisions. They should never allow children to lever the couple against each other either.

It probably goes without saying, that other people, things, and experiences all help formulate who we become as adults as we proceed through our lives. But I would wager that you remember quite well how your parents treated each other.

Have you ever handled your children's situation a certain way, because it is the way your parents handled it when *you* were in a similar situation, when you were under their guidance? Conversely, did you ever say to yourself as a child, I will never do that to my kids?? I imagine you have.

Happy, Loving, Long-Term Relationships generally do not just "happen." They develop over time as men's and women's skills and knowledge develop and grow into genuine intimacy, therefore building loving lasting relationships and becoming best friends at the same time.

Have you ever heard someone say, "I married my best friend?" Isn't that what we all want our spouses to be or become? I know for a fact that my parents were best friends. Looking back, I realize it was a paramount part of why they loved each other so much.

As I will discuss in more detail later, science has discovered huge rational differences between men and women. So, there are things we must learn if we do not already possess the knowledge to have a truly intimate relationship with our spouse.

One is communication skills.

It is one of the crucial things that every marriage needs to be truly intimate. It is really important to know how to use the powerful skill of communication.

This includes being able to tell our loved one what we really mean and getting them to understand what we mean and our point of view, even when they are having a problem doing so. We need to be able to recognize when they don't really get it! And then, we need to be able to come at it from a different direction, better enabling them to understand. All with calm patience.

Also, just as important or maybe even more important is that we need to learn to really listen!

We should try to see things from our partner's point of view. Communication, including listening, is a critical tool for deeper understanding in any kind of relationship. Communication really should always include encouragement and self-correction when needed. We should communicate without the inclusion of anger and hurtful statements that we may not really mean, especially because they can never be taken back.

These are especially crucial *Secrets for a Happy, Loving, Long-Term, Intimate Relationship*. It is a known fact that most women lose the feeling of intimacy when they are stressed, angry or feel attacked or unloved. What is not so known is that many men, although visual and usually easily aroused, can also find their mate much less attractive and many times actually be repulsed by them under the same circumstances.

It is known that the tension and stress from unhappy marriages, or even unhappy friendships, can actually cause illnesses such as cancer. Such tension and stress even shorten a person's life.

So, not only are our own life spans and quality of life negatively affected by poor relationship skills, but we must then consider we usually affect our children's lives also. They suffer or gain from the role models we provide everyday as parents, grandparents, and, in fortunate situations, even as great grandparents.

Therefore, honing the skills of communication can elevate one's life in business, the job market, family life, friendships, and most certainly, intimacy.

 Golf Gimme 3:

I Had No Idea I Was Meeting My Newest Best Friend

In the mid-nineties, I was an amateur and living in California. One day, while playing with some friends of mine at Rolling Hills Country Club, one of the guys said to me, "Why don't you join us and play in the Pro-Am over in Maui in two months? We are playing with the PGA Tour Professionals. It will be a lot of fun to mingle with those guys."

I got the information and decided to fill out the form to go. I had played with the PGA Tour Professionals before and had a nice time. I asked my girlfriend at the time if she wanted to go along. There was no room for her to play, but we could take some time and relax while there. Plus, she could follow along when I played. She loved the idea and agreed to go.

I got to the golf course the first day of the tournament and wondered who I would draw as a professional. Some guys are not all that pleasant to be playing with, but most are.

I drew a professional by the name of Butch Baird. I really did not know a lot about Butch, but when I saw him I recognized him from seeing him on TV. I remembered them saying how he had the best swing on tour. I had absolutely no idea what his personality was like, or what kind of day to expect.

Little did I know that he would become one of my closest male friends in the whole world.

Butch never told me until a few years ago that, when he was taking his golf gear out of his car in the parking lot that day, he had spotted me hitting balls on the range. He said he actually watched me from the parking lot for a while.

He said he noticed I had a lot of good going on in my swing. That meant a lot to me after having learned through the years that Butch has a tremendous eye for the golf swing. Since then, I have heard him tell people that my swing was better than his. He even told me that once.

I know his modesty and could never take that seriously, however, especially knowing how good *his* swing is. Regardless, no greater compliment regarding golf has never been paid to me… especially from a mentor.

Even to this day, he constantly works on his swing. While mine gets worse due to physical problems, today, at age 80, *he* has an even better swing, technically speaking, than he had back in those days when I first met him. At that time he was 10th on the all-time money list.

I had no idea that my future held a professional spot. I had no idea that we would practice together or that he would use my eye to analyze his swing. And I would use *his* extremely refined, highly qualified eye to analyze *my* swing. Best yet, we become best friends at the same time.

Anyway, when I arrived at the first tee on the first day of the tournament, my three playing partners and I shared two carts having two men in each cart. As a professional, Butch had his own cart, which is typical for Pro-Ams. The woman accompanying me was going to follow on foot.

A couple holes later I realize just how friendly and down to earth Butch was. I asked Butch how he would feel about allowing my girlfriend to ride with him. He had talked to her and was very friendly to her, making her feel part of the group.

I Had No Idea I Was Meeting My Newest Best Friend

He responded by saying, "Of course, she can!"

So, she then had a ride for the rest of the round. Plus, she got to know Butch better at the same time.

The next day I drew Doug Ford as my pro. This was a different experience, for sure. He started out very nice, but he began to grow angry towards the end of the round. He felt that the group ahead of us was playing too slowly, and he wanted to make an earlier airline flight. That became his total focus. I hate to admit it, but Doug actually displayed anger by throwing a golf club at one point, still blaming the group ahead of us for his poor shot.

That evening, my girlfriend and I walked into the restaurant for dinner. We immediately noticed Butch and his wife, Pam, sitting at a dinner table. At the same time, he spotted us walking in the door. I waved hello to him, and he motioned for us to come to their table.

We walked over and greeted them, and they asked us to join them for dinner. This was the first time I met his wife and usual caddy, Pam. We were honored to oblige because we had enjoyed meeting him so much.

Later, Butch invited me to visit them at his home in Arizona to stay for a week and play some golf. I was more than thrilled to accept. He and Pam were amazing hosts, and I fell in love with Arizona when I was there.

He introduced me to Desert Mountain Golf Club and encouraged me to buy a home there. The timing was not quite right for me, but I did buy a home there a few years later.

The Practice facilities there were perfect for what was to come for me. Better yet, I was near my newest best friend. The more time we spent together, the more we laughed and built a friendship which will never decline. We are two peas in a prankster pod! I also realized what a special person his wife, Pam, is!

That was really evident, recently, when I had some surgery performed in Scottsdale. I had moved away from the area to accommodate my now ex-wife being able to take care of her sick mother. I was back visiting Arizona when I discovered I needed to go to the hospital. I had planned to stay in a hotel, but Butch and Pam insisted that I stay with them.

Seriously, Butch got up and took me to the hospital at 6 AM, which was a good hour round-trip for him. Then he returned to pick me up and take me back to their home, where Pam made wonderful, healthy meals for us while I recovered. I said "home," because Pam has made it a warm and true "home" and not just a "house." There is a difference. I hope where you live is a home, and not just a house. Is it?

All I can ever think or say about Butch and Pam is how wonderful they always are. I cannot begin to tell you everything that I learned from Butch about golf. He allowed me to suck his brains out at times. It's at times like these that you realize what good friends are really all about. Thank you, Butch and Pam, for your friendship through the years and everything beyond golf, too.

Butch Baird, John Gehrisch, Pam Baird
Par 3 – Hole #7 – Pebble Beach

Hole #4

Are Men Really Brain Dead?

"Love is what we call the situation which occurs when two people who are sexually compatible discover that they can also tolerate one another in various other circumstances."

-- Marc Maihueird
a.k.a. Mark My Word and Anonymous

Hang in here with me on this. It is rather interesting and explains a lot.

Medical research discovered that in the womb, around the eighteenth and twenty-sixth weeks of gestation, something happens that completely changes the males from the females. When using heat-sensitive color monitors, the researchers can actually observe what happens. A chemical bath of different sex-related hormones washes over a baby boy's brain, causing some significant changes that never happen to the brain of a baby girl.

Basically, the human brain is divided into two hemispheres, or halves, each one being connected by a fibrous tissue called the Corpus Collosum. These sex-related chemicals and hormones that flood a baby male's brain will cause the right side of the male's brain to recede slightly, which destroys some of the fibers of the Corpus Collosum that connects the two sides of the brain. As a result, in about 80% of the cases, the male starts life more left-brain-orientated right from birth.

So, what about the females? Because they don't experience the chemical brain bath that the males get, females are much more "global" or "two-sided" in their thinking. Even though electrical impulses can go back and forth from side to side in the male, they are less hindered in the brain of the female and proceed much faster.

You might now be saying that women are right when they call men "brain damaged." I know it sounds like it, but actually what happens in the womb is a miracle of how the male and female adapt in two different ways of thinking. It is one of the main reasons that men and women need each other so much. Assuming they are both truly open to different points of view and able to communicate, they can become an extremely strong team.

The left side of the brain holds the information that is more analytical, logical, and factual, as well as the aggressive centers of thought. About 80% of men hang out in this area of the brain during the majority of their waking hours. It is the section for how to do it, fix it, batting averages, definitions of words, and conquering the trip across country. It is not the romance novel or sensitivity area.

About 80% of females hang out in the right side, typically, where the center for feelings, emotions, primary rational, language, and communication skills reside. Also imagination and enjoyment of fine art or fine music come from there.

Can you see why the differences in interests, talents, and communication skills exist?

It is because of the chemical wash that takes place in the womb. However, the strengths complement each other also. Men and woman actually need each other.

I speak more about these things, including percentages, in Hole 13 – Typical Differences Between Men and Women and Hole 14 – Respecting Differences.

 Golf Gimme 4:

Butch Baird vs Gary Player

Butch shared a story with me about a time when he was playing a tournament in the same group as Gary Player. They had heard that there was a large snake in a pond on the hole they were playing. Having a minute before teeing off, and being inquisitive, Butch decided to cautiously sneak up on the pond and see if he could get a look at this gigantic snake. Step-by-step he slowly approached the pond. Finally he got as close as he thought he might safely want to go. Ever-so-cautiously, he took just one step closer, keeping one leg on the firm ground behind him as he leaned out over the water to get a good view.

Unbeknownst to Butch, Gary had removed his belt from his pants. He quietly snuck up behind Butch and flung the belt around Butch's leg.

Gary's wishes came true as Butch jumped out of the weeds, panicking! His immediate thought was a snake had just hit his leg. Gary stood there laughing at him, and Butch realized he had been on the receiving end of a prank, instead of being the joker himself.

Butch also told me about a time that he and Gary were in the work out trailer that follows the tour. Gary was putting time in on the treadmill.

Butch grabbed a can of the medication that chemically ices down strained muscles. He positioned himself on the machine behind Gary. Because the can is under pressure, he was able to projectile launch some onto Gary's ankle.

Gary immediately felt the cold and looked down at his ankles. Seeing nothing, he looked up towards the ceiling. Seeing nothing there either, he continued his fast walk.

Butch waited a few minutes and repeated his prank, causing Gary, once again, to look down at his ankle and then back up at the ceiling.

When it happened a third time, he called out to the trainer. "Rob, something cold keeps hitting my ankles."

Knowing what was happening, Rob didn't let on.   He simply said, "Gary you must be feeling the cold mist from the air conditioner. It is the Ventura Effect, as the cold air hits the warmer air."

"Oh, okay," said Gary.

He then moved to the stationary bike. Soon after he began concentrating on his workout, Butch also moved to another machine directly behind Gary. Butch again shot cold onto Gary's ankle.

Gary looked down, looked up, looked at Rob, and proclaimed, "Dammit Rob, *it's* following me!"

I still laugh when I think of this. I wish I had been there to witness it first hand, because Gary is so intent during his workouts. He was the one who really started the physical fitness craze that is so prevalent now on tour. He did it long before it became popular. Now players all recognize the benefits.

There was also the time that Butch put a big rock in a competitor's golf bag when he was not looking. The poor guy carried his golf bag through airports with the rock in it for three weeks before discovering it. His poor caddy also carried the bag on the golf course for three weeks, when it wasn't in the cart.

These are only a few of the thousands of stories of fun. We all need to laugh… often.

Hole #5

Dream Delayed

"I should have known something was wrong with my first wife. When I brought her home to meet my parents, they approved of her."
>   -- Woody Allen (1935 -)
>   American actor and filmmaker

One day, my V.P. of Sales and Marketing teamed with my Executive V.P. and pulled me aside.

"John, we think you should take a run at the PGA Tour. We can run the company in your absence. We can contact you if we need to talk about anything."

Well, they knew my heart. At the time, I was living primarily in California. It provided a perfect climate to work on my game.

I thought about their proposal and realized that I had nothing to lose except my pride. I came up with a plan.

I had already been playing some in the Amateur Tour in California, and I had won on Rivera Country Club. This was a great experience, especially because they announced you on the first tee in front of a small gallery, provoking a big case of nerves. I had previously played some in Pro-Ams where they also announced you. Learning to handle your nerves when you know everyone within ear shot was watching proved to be an invaluable skill. All golfers should experience this, if only to get a small sense of what the tour feels like.

My early plan directed me to work on my game for four years, beginning in those amateur tournaments, and then advancing to playing the mini-tours to gain experience.

Then, if I could win on the Mini's, when I turned 50, I could go for my card in what was then called the Senior PGA Tour. The name later would be changed to the Champions Tour. I set my plan to launch on January second of the 1994 New Year.

In early December, my best friend called. Al was also my Vice President, running three manufacturing facilities for me. He shared that he believed that I needed to return to the New England company headquarters. In response to my query as to *why* I needed to change my plans, he said he felt his personal life was interfering with his abilities to do his job, and he was letting me down.

I could not understand how Al could feel that way. I saw our financials every month. We were growing fast and had some of the typical, fast growth-related issues, but we were making good money. Still, I agreed to return. After meeting an obligation to attend a Los Angeles area customer's open house, I assured him I would be back around the week of Christmas.

In September of that year, I recalled standing with him on my deck in Laguna Niguel. With cocktails in hand we watched the sun set over the Pacific and the lights flicker on over Catalina Island. Our friendship was strong.

Al and his wife had three daughters. I was paying for college for one of them, not because he couldn't afford it, but because I was keeping a promise I'd made to him for sticking with me during our earlier tough years.

We had lost money for the first time ever after we purchased a company that had been misrepresented to us. Al knew that we could no longer afford to pay him, and he'd received a job offer for more money. With one daughter going to be heading to college in a few years, this was not a time he could afford to not be earning and saving money.

I understood, but I truly needed him and his expertise. I vowed that if he would stay, we would turn the company around.

Further, if he stayed employed with me, I would pay for her college education. Thankfully, Al chose to back me.

As forecasted, we became profitable again. I was honored to live up to my commitment to him and his daughter.

Now, as we watched the last rays of sunlight disappear, he told me how he and his wife had been sitting alone in their living room just before he'd come west to meet with me. With one daughter away at college and the other two out on dates, he realized it was the first time that he and his wife had been alone together in a very long time.

Al said they had nothing to talk about with each other. He wondered if it was to be their future to just stare at each other. Al added that to that day, when Eileen walked into the room, he still found her to be the most beautiful woman in the world. She was a nice person, but in *my* eyes she was no gorgeous model. To Al, she was perfect.

With sadness, Al shared with me that after twenty-two years of marriage, Eileen had told him that she no longer loved him. She still blamed him for getting her pregnant during college and for her having to drop out. I reminded him that, as of the last time I checked, it took two people to become pregnant. Saying that to *him*, rather than to *her*, did little good.

He went on to say that after the first of the coming year, he saw moving out as his only option with Eileen. He recalled that her parents had lived together for years, not loving each other. Perhaps that was what she expected now, too. However, Al did not see that as an option. We discussed some places he might live if it came to that, but I asked him to think carefully.

It had taken years to reach this crossroad point in their relationship, so it would take time to repair it.

If he wanted to save the marriage, he needed to start immediately. Al wanted to save his marriage, so I gave him a relationships program that I had. I suggested he take it home so he and Eileen could listen and, hopefully, be helped.

Later, he mentioned that I had loaned the program to them previously, which I knew. He had not remembered, but as they started to watch it together, Eileen mentioned that she had watched it the first time that I had loaned it to them. Sadly, he had not had the interest at that time.

Can you see how, if only one person cares, things will only get worse instead of better?

Maybe, if he had realized how serious their problems were back then, he would have watched it the first time.

Notice the communication breakdown here. This is a perfect example of why I include it in my formula. This is critical.

If Eileen had talked to Al about her pent up feelings earlier, maybe they wouldn't have even approached this impasse.

I remember asking Al when the last time was that he'd sent flowers to Eileen for no special reason. He'd answered that he could not remember doing that. I suggested he start there, and he promised he'd try it.

I also asked him if he was sure she was not having an affair. She designed and installed home window treatments. He had told me how she had a big job over three hours away and was arriving home at 3 o'clock in the morning sometimes. That really concerned me. Al assured me that there was no way she would cheat on him.

A few weeks after that conversation on my California deck, he and I spoke again on the telephone about his marriage. I asked if he had sent flowers to her.

"Oh, yeah," he said, "but she got so mad at me!"

"What?!? Why?"

"She was annoyed because I had them delivered to her at work, rather than giving them to her myself," he explained.

"Wow!" I continued, "You have some real serious issues going on here."

I did not connect all the dots at the time. In hindsight, I think she was upset that she'd received the flowers at work. Specifically, it may have annoyed her that they were delivered in the face of the man she would later marry. Interestingly, he also had a home some three hours away.

So, was she having an affair? Was it only a coincidence? I do not know. You decide.

Anyway, I headed back to New England after the open house, as promised. On my first day back, I went to see my friend.

Al's office was a disaster. His desk was piled 18 inches high with papers. Another 18 inches of paper piles towered atop his credenza, too. The floor had papers piled even higher.

Unfortunately, his secretary had resigned some weeks earlier, after realizing she was falling for this married man and could no longer work for him.

As this was the second time such a thing had happened, he decided that we did not need to pay for a secretary. We could save the money, and he could handle the work himself.

Please understand that Al, though a great guy, was no "*GQ*" model. What made him so handsomely attractive to women was his magnetic personality. Women just couldn't help but fall in love with him.

I always had regarded Al as a fair man. Everyone respected him, and no one took advantage or tried to walk all over him. He was exactly the kind of man I was proud to call my friend and have represent me in my business.

Imagine my shock to see his office on this day. I knew he was not making clear decisions. This was one clear sign of stress. Right now, everything to Al was a crisis. Obviously, this was why he wanted me back there.

After some small talk, I decided to roam the plants for the rest of the day to talk with workers. I hoped to get a feel for the problems that my dear friend felt were so out of control.

I found evidence of some expected, typical growing pains. Systems had been outgrown and needed attention. Overall, things were functioning fine, though more cumbersome. Generally, people were also happy.

Thankfully, things were not bad, especially considering our rapid escalation in sales. All things considered, Al and the others reporting to him were doing a great job.

At home that evening, I formed a plan of attack. The following day I walked into Al's office with four empty boxes. I had labeled them: "File," "Delegate," "Important," and "Critical."

Naturally, Al expected everything to go into the "Critical" box. Out of all the many piles in his office, only four things went into the "Critical" box, requiring immediate attention.

I assured him that we would take care of those items the following day. In fact, I took two items, and Al took two items. We did indeed complete them the very next day.

Done! All "Critical" items were gone.

Dream Delayed

We gave out the many things that needed to be delegated to the people who should have been doing them in the first place. I got a couple of the support staff to file things needing filing, which comprised about 75 percent of the piles.

Yeah, right! Al did not need a secretary! Wrong!! Al now had time to take care of the remaining items that we'd placed in the "Important" box with no pressure.

Personally, I had wanted to get a new building into which we could consolidate my three manufacturing facilities to be all under one roof. I worked with a realtor and found one particularly suitable building that I liked.

I grabbed Al to go look at my favorite building option with a contractor one late morning. We discussed my vision and agreed it could be done. Things were looking up. On the way back to work, Al and I stopped for a quick sandwich. As we ate, I spoke candidly to my friend.

"You must be feeling better about things," I started, thinking about how much we had accomplished and how nicely his office was now under control.

Al said, "I feel better about things. I just wish I felt better about the way I feel."

I knew he was still having marital problems. As we were fast approaching Christmas, I chose not to bring up my curiosity over whether or not he may have learned something unsavory about his wife's late night activities three hours away.

Turning thoughts to a brighter subject, I remembered that the New England Patriots, our favorite team, would be in the playoffs on Christmas Eve day. I invited Al to come over that day and watch the game with me.

He said, "That sounds good. I'll probably do that. I just have a couple errands to run first."

Super.

Al hadn't arrived by game time, but I sat down and started watching. As I sat alone, I recalled he'd told me that he had errands to do first.

As time continued to pass by, I thought that it was not like him to not call if he'd decided *not* to come. However, I remembered that he'd also said, "Probably." With the holiday, I realized that he'd likely gotten busy and lost track of time.

Quite frankly, I felt a little ticked off, because I would have changed *my* plans. I'd been invited to the home of a lady I was dating at the time. Now he'd left me to spend Christmas Eve day alone, when I could have been spending it with my lady friend and her family.

When the first game ended, I gave up on Al arriving. I headed to my friend's house to watch the second playoff game and then for dinner.

During dinner, Al's wife called, asking if I'd seen him. He'd told her that he was going to the dry cleaners and then to my house to watch the game. When he didn't come home after the game, she thought that he'd stayed for the second game, but that was over now, and she still couldn't reach him.

Had he been in an accident? My mind started thinking the worst.

Eileen added that Al had spoken of checking himself into the hospital Depression Unit. She'd driven there, but she had not seen his company car. Because of confidentiality laws, no one at the hospital would give her any information either.

She'd even driven to the bus station, but his car was not there either. Eileen was at her wits' end and did not know what to do. I assured her that I would come right over and help find him.

I called my son, who also worked at the company. He started checking with all the hotels and drove by our company facilities. I went by the apartment complex which I had discussed with Al as a residential possibility for the New Year. I also started calling all the hospitals.

Naturally, no one would tell me anything either. I explained the problem. I said, "Do not tell me if he is there or not. Just tell me, if you were me, would you continue to look for him or not?"

Reluctantly, they all advised that, if they were me, they'd continue to search.

At about 3:30 in the morning, we gave up. I called Eileen. I assured her that I would meet her later in the morning to go with her to file a missing person report, as the 24-hour waiting period would be up. I went to bed.

Later, while eating breakfast, I kept pondering where Al could be. We'd searched for his car everywhere.

While thinking of our company facilities, I realized there was no way to hide a car inside as all the facilities only had truck height loading doors. However, we had just rented a new building that did have one ground floor loading door. My son had looked there. Having no key and seeing no sign of the car, he'd moved on.

Now I called my plant manager and asked him to meet me to give me the key. Naturally, he asked why I had such urgency on Christmas morning. I explained.

I insisted that he stay with his family, but he refused. Al was his friend, too. We were all very concerned.

The plant manager, my son, and I all arrived at the facility within seconds of each other. As the overhead door slowly rose, my heart broke. More than twenty years later, I have tears in my eyes just remembering the moment I knew I'd lost my dear friend, Al.

A white hose was attached to the car's tail pipe. It wrapped around the car and entered the passenger-side window, where he had stuffed his dry cleaning to seal off the opening around the hose in the window opening.

My best friend had ended his marital problems. And everything else.

Once the police had determined that this was not a homicide, I was released to go tell his family that a loving husband and father was never coming home again. I know I could have handled this mission better. To this day I wish that I had.

How *do* you find the right words at a time like that?

I believe that Al wanted me there to handle it for him. I think that is a large part of the reason he called me back to New England. Al had thought everything out so well. He had bought a hose clamp to make sure the hose did not vibrate off the tail pipe. He even had the clothes, supposedly for the dry cleaner, to seal off the gaps in the window.

He'd given us the weekend to take care of the car and give the plant time to air out. The car had run out of gas, exhausting all the fumes and leaving an awful odor.

We never did tell the workers what had happened in that facility. No one but the three of us that found him ever knew.

After we buried her husband, Eileen and I shared a drink one afternoon. I explained to her that we usually go through four stages during grief. One of those stages was anger.

I said, "I never thought I could be angry with Al, but I kind of am."

She chimed in, "Boy, I sure am, too!" I inquired for more information to try and understand what was going through her head.

She replied, "I had it good, and he has taken that away from me."

I was in shock. She was referring to the way of life he'd provided for her.

I wanted to say, "Too bad you did not tell him that before he took his own life." However, I knew at that point it would serve no purpose except to vent my anger and be hurtful, and I did not want to hurt her. So, I said nothing.

We soon discovered that Al's mother had been treated for depression for two years, but she had felt embarrassed and didn't tell anyone. Two of his brothers also had depression treatment after we lost Al.

Depression is not to be ignored. We all need to learn to recognize the signs.

Al's words over our last lunch together haunt me to this day. "I feel better about things. I just wish I felt better about the way I feel." I never in my wildest dreams realized from those words what was to follow.

Later, I was looking at photos I had taken of Al. I had never noticed before that I only had one photo of him where he was smiling. I think if a person is happy inside, then they will likely smile in photos most of the time. Some will smile anyways, but this was so telling about Al, if I had only noticed.

Al and I also loved to play golf together. Thinking back, I only remember specifics of one round together. The rest are a blur of just being happy we were together. I beat Al almost every time we played, even after giving him a handicap. In hindsight, I so wish I had given him more strokes so he would have won more. Maybe that could have helped make him feel better about himself, so he could have been happier inside. As competitive as I am, looking back, winning meant nothing to me when compared with my love for this man. I wish like anything that I could go back and do it over.

I think it was Jack Nicklaus's father whole told him something like, "Knowing how to be a *good winner* is only a fraction as important as knowing how to be a *good loser*. Initially, I thought I understood what he meant. But I now think, whether intentional or not, it is deeper than I had realized.

Looking back, I don't remember one specific win over Al, but I will never forget Al. I wish I had lost more frequently to him. It's too late for me to change that. But maybe this will help make you evaluate the "real" importance of your life, when involving relationships.

The only specific thing I remember in a round of golf with Al was that I was with him when he achieved his *only* lifetime "hold in one." I remember it like it was yesterday, though it was 30 years ago. He hit a driver up the hill into a strong wind on hole number 16 at the Manchester Country Club, and it went into the cup. They buried Al with that ball.

I had not seen the signs. Depression can be caused by many things. It is obvious that there was a chemical imbalance going on within Al's family. The collapse of his marriage did not cause his depression, but it certainly pushed him over the edge.

Seek treatment if you have such feelings. Encourage loved ones and friends to seek treatment if you ever see the signs. Don't embarrass them, but rather, encourage them to talk about it.

Later, in fact, I recognized signs that concerned me with another employee. One day I held this grown man in my arms as he openly wept. He told me that he loved his job and loved his family, but he was not happy and did not know what to do. I got him into treatment before it was too late. *His* story has a happy ending. I only wish I knew earlier what I know now, so that I could have saved my best friend.

Maybe you can help someone in your life. If you do, and my sharing has helped, I will consider this book to have been completely worthwhile.

 Golf Gimme 5:

Double Double Eagle

A number of years ago, I was to play my regular golf course for summer months, called the Lake Winnipesaukee Golf Club (LWGC). For much of my adult life I had a summer home in the Lakes region of New Hampshire on the State's largest lake, Lake Winnipesaukee.

I had just joined this newly renovated course. LWGC was built on many acres, and on almost every hole, you could not see any of the other holes. Every hole had either woods, hills, creeks, or marsh or all of them lining the fairways on whichever hole you were playing.

This was nice in that you never once got the feeling that you were playing a hole that you had already played. Each one looked so different, unlike so many other golf courses. You always had to hit the ball pretty straight, or you could pay the price by losing a ball and receiving one or two penalty strokes.

Playing this golf course in the autumn with the fall foliage in the trees was a real treat also. As you may know, people come from all over the world to New England just to see the fall foliage. I have read that as many as 2 or 3 million people have visited New Hampshire in given years to see the foliage.

The state is the only one left with no sales tax nor state income tax. They do impose a tax on hotel rooms and restaurant meals, obviously targeting the many tourists that visit in different seasons of the year.

Anyway, I had only played the men's club championship at LWGC one year, when it was played as a gross champion. I happened to win that year.

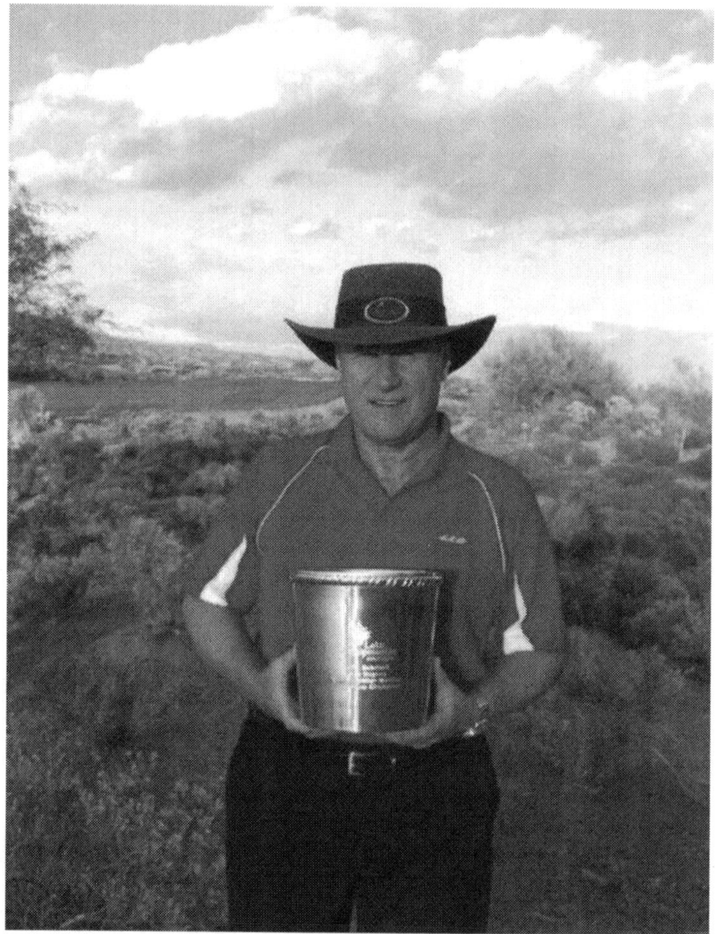

John Gehrisch with LWGC championship trophy

I hold the course record at a couple golf clubs. One was there, at the Lake Winnipesaukee Golf Club. That record may still stand. I am not sure.

On this particular day, I met some guys to play and teed it up on the first hole. The first hole is a par four, and I happened to drive it onto the green. I had about a 15-foot putt for eagle and drained it.

The next hole is a par five. I hit a driver and the three-wood pin high to the right and just off the green. I hit a good chip, and the ball ended in the cup for a second eagle in a row.

In all my years of golf, I do not remember ever having two eagles back to back like that, and certainly not on holes one and two.

I had been talked into representing the club at an Inter-Club Tournament Match being held at Bald Peak Colony Club four days later. My match was the top match, and so we drew to begin on Hole number one.

This was a par four, down the hill, with trees on both sides, and with mounds where many people would hit their drives. It was very hard to save par from those mounds because there was a very high rough growing on the mounds.

I had been a member at this club for a while, so I'd learned through the years that the good percentage shot was to simply hit an iron off the tee. This helped in avoiding the mounds, leaving just a wedge onto the green.

On this particular day, I decided to be aggressive. I hit my driver and cleared the mounds on the fly rolling up just inches from the middle front of the green. I can't remember if I putted or chipped the ball, but it went into the cup for an eagle.

The second hole happens to be a par five through the woods, very much like holes at the Lake Winnipesaukee Golf Club. I hit a great drive down the middle and ripped the three wood, landing six feet short of the pin in the middle of the green. I made the putt for a second eagle in row.

Needless to say, perhaps my competitors were in shock at having two eagles thrown at them on the first two holes, and being two down so quickly, even after their handicap strokes were applied, reducing their scores.

The rest of the Match was pretty much mine. In other words they probably felt like they had drawn Tiger Woods to play against and were pretty well beaten after two holes.

I'd never before seen that happen in all the golf I played in match play.

As I said, I don't remember ever having two Eagles in a row in my entire life. And suddenly, I not only had two Eagles in a row, but I had two eagles in a row two times in one week, only four days apart.

What makes this more exceptional, is that I had it on Hole number one, then Hole number two, a par four and a par five, on two different golf courses.

These are the kinds of things that make golfers fall in love with the game.

Hole #6

Using Kids as Pawns

"Whenever I date a guy, I think, is this the man that I want my children to spend their weekends with?"

- Rita Rudner (1953 -)
American comedian, writer, and actress

Wow, do I hate it when I see people use their children as pawns against their spouse to get even during or after a divorce?!!? How cruel can someone be?

No matter what their feelings are for their spouse, they still are the father or mother of their children. How dare they use them to hurt their spouse!!?! What did the children do to deserve that? How will it affect them the rest of their lives?

Many times the person who has primary custody will constantly bad mouth their spouse, hoping to get the kids to hate them, too. If they are successful in driving a wedge between them, then the children are truly from a completely broken home. They may unnecessarily lose one parent forever in their life, and also grandparents.

I have seen it happen so many times. It is so hurtful and done with malice that has no regard for the best interest of the children, only for the selfish, self-centered person.

If you have done this, I beg you to reconsider. Maybe it is not too late to repair the damage that is being done. You don't have to rekindle things with your ex, just be a better person and allow your kids not to have to suffer a divorce also.

Later I will show you that children are four times more likely to divorce when they come from a broken home. Don't do that to your kids.

Give *them* a fighting chance to be happy.

I was married the first time when I was barely 19 years old. Yes, I know, trust me, you do not have to tell me how stupid I was.

By the way, this book would be a great gift idea for any young adults that you love.

We had children when we were still kids ourselves, but, at the time, we thought we were grownups. All and all, I think our kids were lucky, looking back, as I think we did a pretty good job of being parents when they were younger, especially considering that we had no training other than watching our own parents be parents. But then, isn't that pretty much how we all do it?

Yes, I will give my ex-wife credit where credit is due. She was a good wife and mother for many years.

I have often thought, and what is really amazing to me is, we go through Grade School, High School, and often College, and I have yet to find one person who had even one class on what may be the two most important things we do in our existence on earth. Those being how to choose a life mate and how to raise children, if we decide to have them.

I am trying to assist on the first in this book. When I realized how much our examples influence our kids, I realized that not only this Chapter might help the children, but maybe the whole book, too.

I have an extremely close friend who had his children used against him during his divorce. He has not heard from his two daughters in something like 12 years or more. Yes, his wife turned them against him.

Like anyone, he is not perfect, but he <u>is</u> a really good person. He is someone his kids should both know and of whom they should be proud.

They basically heard only one side at home… their mother's.

They were young teenagers when the divorce happened.   I think they also wanted their time on the weekend to date, so they were happy to limit him so their weekends were free to do what *they* selfishly wanted, instead of spending time with their father.

After all, when we are young, we tend to live in our own little worlds. Often, young adults are too self-centered if they don't have the proper guidance. Later in life, we often wish we would have done things differently. I know I certainly have.

Meanwhile, he and they have lost forever many important years. He has been unfairly deprived of participating in important events in their lives, and they have missed having a true father in their lives. Children were meant to have two support mechanisms in their life: a mother and father. Only having one when it is not necessary is a shame.

I have advised him a little and suggested he have patience. There is not a lot a father can do until he is welcome again in their lives, as they are young adults. He cannot force them to love him again. He can only wait and hope that once they mature more, they will reach back out to him.

At one point, my son and I went through what we now jokingly refer to as our "Black Out Period." I waited.

Fortunately, he reached out to me when he was ready. To this day we probably have a difference of opinion as to what started it. That really does not matter. What matters is that we were always best buds, and we are again.

In our case, both his sister and his wife were instrumental in him coming back to me. We both owe them a debt of gratitude. Thank you to Lysa and Julie.

Of course, there are exceptions to it being in the best interest of the children to have both parents in their lives. And, of course, common sense needs to be used.

I believe the children should make the choice. However, the choice should not be influenced by a biased spouse.

For example, in my first marriage, over time, my ex changed. She became verbally abusive to the whole family.

I remember sitting at the dinner table and listening to her ranting and raving. Then one of her friends called on the phone. She would answer, "Oh, *HI!*" She was suddenly warm and friendly, as if another person had just come out of nowhere. The rest of us would just look at each other in disbelief.

Another quirk was that she insisted that people take their shoes off at the door when we had visitors.

Needless to say, most people did not come to visit more than once. She would quickly rake any footprints that appeared in the carpet, making people feel uncomfortable that they had even made an imprint. She was an obsessive person in this regard.

Don't get me wrong. I am all for a clean home. I have always had one. But I think my father put it best when he told her one time, "Congratulations, Cindy. You have done a great job of turning this home into a house!"

Think about it. It was brilliant. It is great advice.

Make your house, a home, not the other way around.

My daughter was after me for 10 years to leave and take her and my son with me. I told her I thought my ex was going through an early change of life, and we needed to be patient and supportive.

My daughter said, "Dad, we studied that in school. A change of life does not last 12 years!"

She made me laugh, but she also made me think. Still, divorce was not yet in my vocabulary. I was there for better or worse. And things got worse and worse for us all as time went on.

I was uneducated and did not realize that once kids are old enough, for which the age is determined by the state in which you live, the children can decide with whom they live in a marital breakup.

Hands down, both would have chosen to live with me. I felt it was better to endure, than to take a chance they might have to live with my ex without me there to at least help them.

As a teenager, my son, who is one of the most mild-mannered people I know, who cannot even spell the word "anger," was twice driven by his mother to the point where he put his fist through a wall of my home. My daughter was threatened with a knife to her throat one day when I was at work.

Another day when I was working, I came home to discover that she had permanently kicked our son out of the house. He was moving out in a couple of weeks anyway, so I knew that he would adjust quickly, but she had not even called to discuss it with me. Our relationship was so troubled by that time that I knew if I did not back her decision there would be hell to pay.

After we did leave, my daughter had to go back home once for a couple weeks, while I moved closer to her school. She was a cheerleader, and I did not want her driving far at night by herself after games.

While she was back home, my ex and her sister, surrounded her in a chair and yelled into her face for over 30 minutes.

After she was able to return to me, I found this out. I promised her that she would *never* have to step foot in that house again!

Twice my ex tried to hit me with her fist and threw my parents' glass ash tray at me. Fortunately, she did not connect with any of these. The first time I warned her that I would not tolerate such behavior and that I would leave.

The second time it happened I left, and I never went back.

After I left, she did put her fist right through the screen of the lake house door, while I was standing on the porch showing her on a piece of paper that indicated she was in violation of the usage schedule she, herself, had prepared for the court, since we were splitting time at the lake house I had purchased for us. It was my week to use it and not hers.

As I stood on the porch looking and pointing at the usage schedule that her own attorney had given the court, her fist flew through the screen of the door and connected with my chin. I did not see that punch coming, but I was not hurt.

As much as I wanted to pull her through the screen door and throw her off the porch, she knew that I would never touch her. She used that to her advantage.

Keeping my composure, I ultimately won the day by threatening to call the police if she was not out within thirty minutes. She knew that I was not bluffing, so she left.

I was later told that this was the second-worst divorce case that my attorney ever handled. Five days of trial ensued, when all we had to do was sit down and divide things evenly.

In my ex's infinite desire to fight instead of talk, it cost us $1-million just to divorce. That was money for which I had worked hard. We could have enjoyed the money and passed it on to our children.

I was willing to give her the half of everything to which she was entitled by law. But she wanted it all. Greed is an amazing thing to watch.

She ripped through five attorneys during the two-year process. They kept quitting on her because she was impossible to deal with.

Meanwhile, she actually went around the town in which we lived telling people that the reason my daughter went with me was because we were having an affair!

It is one thing to lie about your husband, which she did constantly, but to say such a hurtful thing about your own daughter is downright sick.

I told my kids that I did not want the divorce to be the reason they did not have a relationship with their mother. I tried very hard to never once put her down in front of them. I figured that they could decide their future with her.

I even suggested during the divorce proceedings that my ex choose four counselors to help out. I then talked my daughter into choosing one of those.

I paid for the session, and in the middle of the first session, my ex got up and walked out because she did not like what the counselor was saying to her. And this was one of the counselors that *she* had chosen! That was the first and last session.

One other time, some years after, my daughter reached out to her, only to have more head games attempted. Neither my son nor my daughter have anything to do with her to this day, almost 30 years later.

I am so proud of the way my kids have rebounded from what they went through. They have become strong adults, but I can see scars pop up occasionally in all of us.

Hind sight is 20/20, but I should have left earlier for so many reasons. FYI, I stayed in the marriage for 22 years, so I gave it a lot.

Sometimes you need to realize that no matter *how* many times you hit your head against a wall, the wall will win, and it is time to give in before your head does.

After all I went through, I did receive one of my most cherished gifts. It is a letter that my daughter wrote to me when she was in college. I am going to share it here. I hope she will forgive my loving indulgence.

It shows that kids *do* see what you try to do. Even if they may not appreciate it at the time, there's a good chance that they might later.

I tear up to this day when I read it. Maybe you can see why I am so proud of my kids.

I include a typed version after the photographs of the original handwritten note, if you prefer. I hope you will agree, that when a daughter says words like these to her father, he cannot possibly have a bad day… or life!

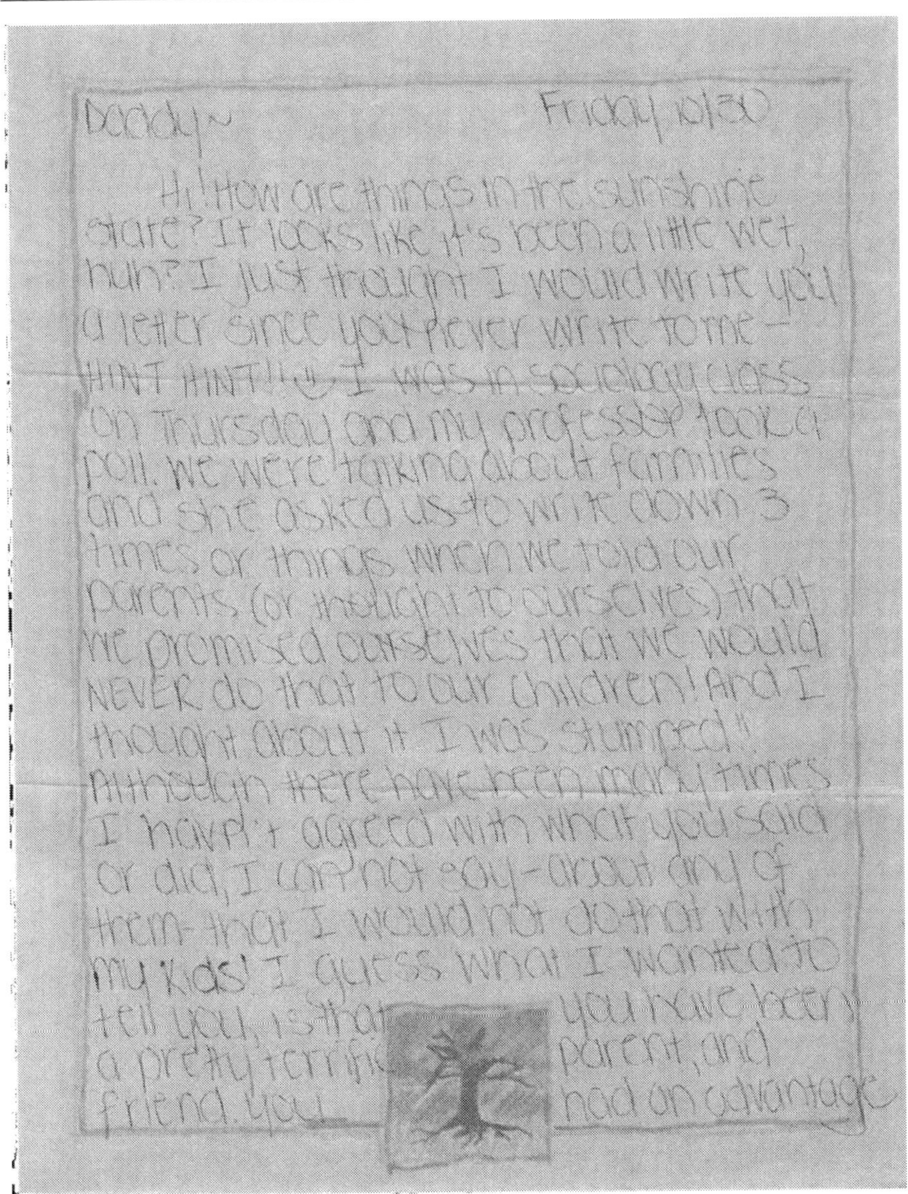

Daddy~   Friday 10/30
        Hi! How are things in the sunshine
state? It looks like it's been a little wet,
huh? I just thought I would write you
a letter since you never write to me—
HINT HINT!! :) I was in sociology class
on Thursday and my professor took a
poll. We were talking about families
and she asked us to write down 3
times or things when we told our
parents (or thought to ourselves) that
we promised ourselves that we would
NEVER do that to our children! And I
thought about it I was stumped!!
Although there have been many times
I haven't agreed with what you said
or did, I cannot say—about any of
them—that I would not do that with
my kids! I guess what I wanted to
tell you, is that   you have been
a pretty terrific   parent, and
friend. You   had an advantage

though, because you had such wonderful parents as role models! If that had anything to do with it, I guess Andy and I will be good parents too. But you also had a major disadvantage as far as I was concerned! And it was my fault. I put unfair demands on you. I expected you to not only play father to me, but mother too. The thing is, somewhere along the way — you became much more than either one. You became my friend.

You have always given me so many things — and I know I am spoiled. But being my friend is the most important gift you ever gave me. And I don't think I have ever said thank you. You have taught me good values and my judgement is slowly improving. Again because of you. Our family has been lucky because you have worked so hard and always provided for us — no matter what mom claims. Although she has taken many of the material things you earned, she can never take away your accomplishments!!!

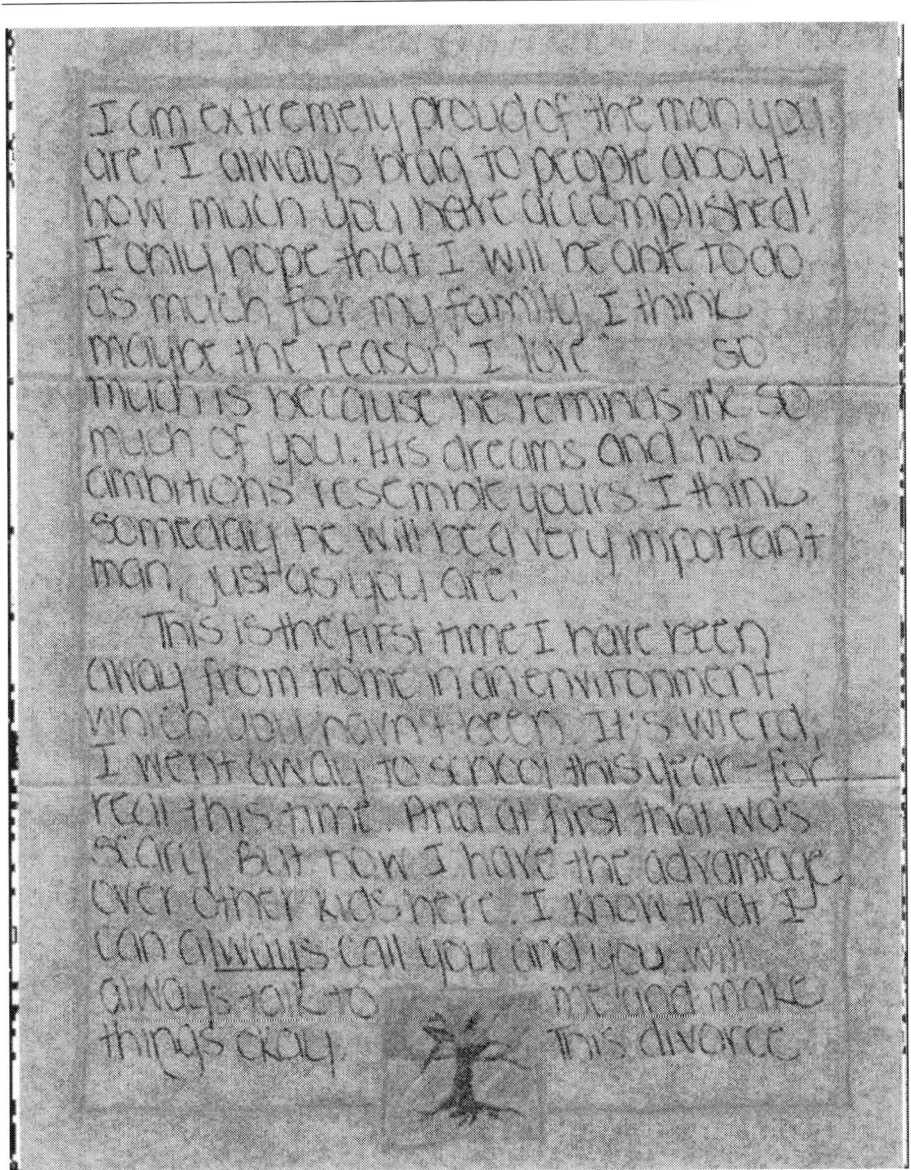

I am extremely proud of the man you are! I always brag to people about how much you have accomplished! I only hope that I will be able to do as much for my family. I think maybe the reason I love _____ so much is because he reminds me so much of you. His dreams and his ambitions resemble yours. I think someday he will be a very important man, just as you are.

This is the first time I have been away from home in an environment which you haven't been. It's weird. I went away to school this year—for real this time. And at first that was scary. But now I have the advantage over other kids here. I knew that I can always call you and you will always talk to _____ me and make things okay. _____ This divorce was very hard on all of us. People usually say the children suffer the most. But they didn't have you as a father. (Nah nah! ☺) It was hard for me, but you made sure it was as easy for me as it could be. And in turn you took the suffering. That deserves plenty of admiration!

I only have one thing left to say. Promise me you will not ever settle for second best again. If you love someone and they are all you need to make you happy, that is what is important. And I promise I will love her too. But if you need more than they can give you, you go find it. You are an exceptional person - one of a kind. You should have that in return - NO LESS!!

Well, I guess I just wanted you to know all of this. And in case I haven't said so in awhile, I love you very much! I just thought it was time someone told you how special you are. And time I said thank you!!! Take care of you!!

All My Love, Lysa

Daddy –

Hi! How are things in the sunshine state? It looks like it's been a little wet, huh? I just thought I would write you a letter since you never write to me – HINT HINT!! ☺

I was in sociology class on Thursday and my professor took a poll. We were talking about families and she asked us to write down 3 times or things when we told our parents (or thought to ourselves) that we promised ourselves that we would NEVER do that to our children! And I thought about it. I was stumped!! Although there have been many times I haven't agreed with what you said or did, I cannot say – about any of them – that I would not do that with my kids!

I guess what I wanted to tell you, is that you have been a pretty terrific parent, and friend.

You had an advantage though, because you had such wonderful parents as role models. If that had anything to do with it, I guess Andy and I will be good parents too. But you also had a major disadvantage as far as I was concerned! And it was my fault.

I put unfair demands on you. I expected you to not only play father to me but mother too. The thing is, somewhere along the way – you became much more than either one. You became my friend.

You have always given me so many things – and I know I am spoiled. But being my friend is the most important gift you ever gave me. And I don't think I have ever said thank you. You have taught me good values and my judgment is slowly ☺ improving. Again because of you.

Our family has been lucky because you have worked so hard and always provided for us – no matter what mom claims. Although she has taken many of the material things you earned, she can never take away your accomplishments!!!

I am extremely proud of the man you are! I always brag to people about how much you have accomplished! I only hope that I will be able to do as much for my family.

I think maybe the reason I love my boyfriend so much is he reminds me so much of you. His dreams and his ambitions resemble yours. I think someday he will be a very important man, just as you are.

This is the first time I have been away from home in an environment which you haven't been. It's weird, I went away to school this year – for real this time. And at first that was scary.

But now I have the advantage over other kids here. I know that I can <u>always</u> call you and you will always talk to me and make things okay.

This divorce was very hard on all of us. People usually say the children suffer the most. But they didn't have you as a father. (Nah Nah! ☺) It was hard for me, but you made sure it was as easy for me as it could be. And in turn you took the suffering! That deserves plenty of admiration!

I only have one thing left to say. Promise me you will not ever settle for second best again. If you love someone and they are all you need to make you happy, that is what is important. And I promise that I will love her too.

But if you need more than they can give you, you go find it. You are an exceptional person – one of a kind. You should have that in return – NO LESS!!

Well, I guess I just wanted you to know all of this. And in case I haven't said so in a while, I love you very much!

I just thought it was time someone told <u>you</u> how special you are.

And time I said thank you!! Take care of you!!

All my love,

Lysa

 Golf Gimme 6:

Preparing to Play Professionally

I sold my main company in mid-1999. I was six years behind my original plan to go for my card to play the tour. I was averaging between a negative 4 and a negative 6 handicap.

Many golfers, even those who play a lot, do not realize that handicaps are the opposite of what you expect. A negative handicap does not mean you average negative scores below par for the golf courses you play.

It actually means you exceed par on average. And a plus handicap means you're averaging under par.

A golf handicap is not simple. It actually is a multiple step process. I'm only going to touch briefly on this. You can get more detail on the Internet if you're interested.

1. You first need a minimum of five scores on the 18-hole rounds or 10 nine-hole scores to calculate the adjusted gross score (AGS), and you only use a portion of your *best* scores, not all scores.

2. Once you have the AGS, you use it to determine your handicap differential.

3. Then you can calculate your handicap index by multiplying by .96.

4. Each golf course is rated for difficulty and is assigned a slope and rating to represent that to differentiate them. By using the slope and rating, you then can determine your handicap for that given golf course

I set out a plan of attack trying to be realistic. I knew that a negative handicap was not even close to being good enough to play the tour.

Tour players do not maintain a handicap because they are always playing gross score tournaments. Amateurs typically play net score tournaments using their handicap to reduce their score to some adjusted number closer to par. Players on tour probably would range from a +4 to possibly as good as +8. Maybe a few would be even better than that at certain times in their career.

I knew I had to be realistic with my plan, or I was kidding myself. I had to reach at least a +3 to even think about playing professionally. I knew that I needed to be at least a +3 to even play on the mini tours with any success, let alone the Champions Tour, which was my ultimate goal.

Having lost all the time gaining previous experience, I was not motivated to live out of the bags for 25 weeks a year. But I still wanted to get in behind the ropes on the big tour. I wanted to do that for my dad even more than myself.

So, I set my first goal to become a +3. If I could do that, I would play on the mini tours for experience. I knew that if I could not win on the mini tours, I had no business even thinking about the Champions Tour. In my mind, I felt it would take me six months to become a legitimate +3, and that was only possible if I worked on it like the full-time job that it was. I was surprised and pleased that it only took me three months with a diligent work ethic.

I would begin the day working out with a golf-oriented physical trainer first thing every morning during the week. I would then go work my short game until noon, including putting, chipping, and bunker play.

I would take a break and get something to eat and then return to the range and hit a minimum of one pyramid of balls (over 200 balls). If I was working on something specific I would hit 1½, and, on rare occasions, even two pyramids.

I would then go play 18 holes with two golf balls, finishing at dark 5 to 6 days a week. I was very fortunate to be practicing out of Desert Mountain Golf Club, because it has some of the best practice facilities in the country, including six Jack Nicklaus Signature golf courses, for variety.

In my opinion, one problem many players have when hitting that many balls on the range, is they will hit ball after ball with the same golf club. That is not typical of the way it works on the golf course. Many times, I would try to replicate the true golfing experience on the course. I would actually have a match with myself to also add some pressure. I would determine an imaginary fairway on the range, based on certain landmarks. I would hit with my driver, and if I hit the ball in the fairway, I could continue. If I missed it, I lost the hole.

I would then pick one of the several practice greens that were laid out in the practice range at different distances. I would choose a different green with a different distance for each imaginary hole I was playing.

If I hit the green with my next iron shot, I would win the hole. Every third hole I would add a par five where I had to hit a fairway wood into my imaginary fairway after the driver.

If I hit all three shots into the targets, I would win the hole. If I missed any one of those shots, I would lose the hole. It was a great practice regimen and helped me a lot to hone my golf skills to prepare for the tour. You might want to consider such a practice procedure yourself.

I would also occasionally play in a couples' event on Sunday with my then wife.

It was actually pretty funny when I had to explain to couples playing with us, that instead of *subtracting* strokes for my handicap like they did, I had to *add* strokes to my score. No one seemed very happy about that. LOL

Once I had reached the +3 handicap, it became a bad round for me to shoot par. I decided to turn professional and began playing as many mini tour events as I could get into, just to see if I could win.

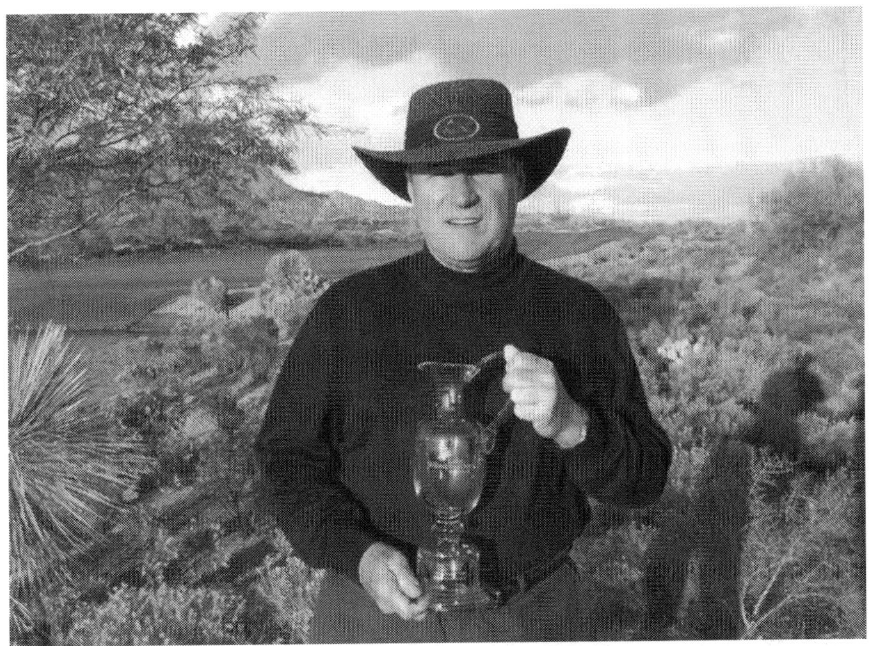

John Gehrisch on Western Pro Tour

Once people turn professional, there's no real reason to maintain a handicap, so I stopped also. I really have no idea how much better than a +3 that I actually got, but I do know that I improved it.

A very small percentage of people in this country have a plus handicap, so most golfers do not understand it. I read somewhere that someone with a single digit *negative* handicap was in the top 10% of the country in ability. I have no idea what a single digit <u>plus</u> handicap would mean, but I know it's extremely rare.

The USGA states that 5.13% of players have a -9 to 9.9 index. Handicap is calculated off your index, but usually it is close to the same when you get down to single-digit indexes. Only .92% have a +1 or better. I have no idea where a +3 falls. Obviously, it is less than .92% and probably a lot less.

Regardless, I did lousy a number of times on the mini tour, but who likes to talk about that? LOL

I took second place a couple times before finally breaking through and winning my first tournament on the Western States Senior Tour.

So, in late 1999, I decided to start trying to join the Champions Tour, beginning as a Monday qualifier at the MasterCard Mexican Open in Mexico.

And so it begins!

Hole #7

All Couples Fight

Photo credit: More Funny Stuff @ MegaLawtz.com

The difference between fighting/arguing and discussing is,
usually when you fight/argue, you do not listen to your partner.
In other words, you only listen to yourself talking and
think about the next point you want to make to support your point of view.
Therefore, you don't truly even consider your
partner's point of view or needs, as you would in a discussion.
-- John A. Gehrisch
American Entrepreneur and Tour Golf Professional

I have heard people say many times that all couples have fights. Really? Maybe you need to have told my parents that. In the 45 years I remember knowing them they did not fight even once.

Maybe we first need to establish and agree on the meaning of a "fight," since it can mean very different things to different people. If to you fight means "disagree," then I would have to concur with that.

But if you mean "quarrel," then I would not concur. Of course, my parents discussed things and had differences of opinion. But it was always done calmly and respectfully.

Personally, I was in a long-term relationship with a wonderful lady, and we never fought or quarreled one time. We could discuss our points of view, and we both respected and loved each other enough to listen and consider the other's point of view. Sometimes one of us would convince the other that they were right. We both had open minds and realized that no one is always right.

Sometimes we would not totally agree. In those situations we would find a way to meet someplace in the middle where we both could live with the result.

It is rare, if you calmly think about things, that you find something that is so important that you need to dig your heels in and not budge for someone for whom you have love and feelings.

Looking back, this was the most peaceful relationship in my life. Everyone thought we would marry. It did not happen for other reasons, but in my definition of fighting, there was not one fight or quarrel in many, many years.

I learned from this how important choosing the right person is in the first place. That means a person who is like me, or compatible, not my opposite.

I realize we hear that opposites attract. If you want to marry a magnet, then listen to them. But if you want a truly *Happy, Loving, Long-Term Relationship*, then please listen to me about this.

This is not a situation where opposites attract.

It's not that opposites cannot live together, or marry one another and stay married. If all or most of the other components in the formula that I will disclose are present, it is possible for an opposite type couple to stay married for a long time. But there may be times when they will want to kill each other.

I have seen such marriages, where people would die for each other, even while being opposites.

But if you want true harmony, do not marry an opposite. It is taking a huge chance and stacking the odds strongly against you.

As a litmus test to what I have just said, ask yourself, "Are my close friends similar to or opposite from me? Do they share similar views and interests with me or do they do things that I despise or find distasteful?"

Here's another example. If you are a staunch conservative, do you tend to hang out with liberals? Or, if you are a dedicated liberal, do you tend to hang out with conservatives? Certainly we all tend to have friends that are opposites in some respects, but are they people with whom you would want to live day-in and day-out for the rest of your life? I think if you are honest, you will say, "No." That said, why would you want to marry an "opposite?"

So, my answer is, **NO WAY** do *all* couples fight! I know from personal experience, a non-argumentative person will not be truly happy with someone who is argumentative. So, if you are not argumentative, seek the same for a *Happy, Loving, Long-Term Happy Relationship.*

But let's say you find yourself in a relationship where anger and fights do exist. Even many healthy couples can find anger in their relationship. It is preferable if you can avoid it in the first place, but sometimes personalities won't allow it. So, what do you do?

First it needs to be short-term anger.

Letting hurt feelings drag on and on not only damages a relationship, it can be fatal. Why? Because, if anger is not dealt with, it will act like a battery acid that eats away at metal. It will eat away at the couple's relationship and eventually destroy it.

Most of the time, it really is *not* that we are upset with the other person in the first place. Rather, we are upset with ourselves.

A couple needs to keep the "spirit of openness" with each other. In terms of dealing with anger in a constructive way, this enables them to later discuss things calmly. That alone helps them take gigantic strides forward towards intimacy.

Those who fail each other in dealing with hurt feelings and frustration, are shoving their relationship into a darkness where it can spiral down into major pitfalls. Eventually, it can reveal dangerous obstacles that may not be overcome.

Remember that it can take up to a year for a power struggle to show up in a relationship, so take your time to see if pops up its ugly head. Then see how you and your mate handle it. When a power struggle exists, it indicates a struggle for "who's is command."

It not uncommon for a spouse or dating partner to go along with the other's every wish for a year or some time period. But, after time has passed, they may suddenly reach the point where they will no longer give up what they consider to be their rights. They begin to use emotional "rights and lefts" to make their points, to try and change the other person, or to alter their relationship.

When thrown into a power struggle, suddenly everything seems to become an issue. Really, it is all the little things building up and attaching to everything that moves.

Should this continue, they can digress to the next level. Now the battle becomes over someone needing to change or someone needing to be in control, or else the whole thing will implode. They both start to dig in their heels, causing a death grip on the relationship.

Next, one person, if not both, begins to question why they are in the relationship in the first place. Is it all worth it? Should they stay?

When that happens, one very important part of the formula discussed later is destroyed… namely security!

Everything escalates in this level. This is where everything is blown out of proportion, and things like not putting the cap on the toothpaste become grounds for divorce.

There is a way to break free from this vicious cycle. We can deal with anger more constructively when we consider three contributing factors.

1. If we feel a person is devaluing us, or blocking our goals and objectives, it often sparks anger.

2. If we devalue our partner, it results in guilt feelings within us, burning us up emotionally inside.

3. If we feel a person is tossing us away for another person, or something has become more important than we are, we harbor feelings of abandonment or rejection. This can cause deep resentment and pain within us, sometimes even causing knots in our stomach from the anxiety.

Sometimes we purposely offend our significant other by our words or deeds. That can close off their spirt to us. They can do it to us, also causing *us* to close *them* out without even being conscience of the fact.

When a person is open in spirt, that person's mind is open. This represents that the person is free of anger, which displays a willingness to communicate and listen to ideas and thoughts.

They are also open to being in the presence of others and open to the touch of loved ones. That is the state to which we want to recover.

Examples of how we can close off someone's spirit include:

- Harsh tone of voice
- Harsh words
- Criticizing unjustifiably
- Making them feel like they or their opinion do not have value
- Taking them for granted
- Making sarcastic remarks
- Making jokes about their physical appearance, family, or character
- Forcing them to do something they are not comfortable doing
- Being suspicious of someone who is not deserving
- Being disrespectful to them, especially in front of others
- Not acknowledging when we are wrong, even when we are

A closed spirit is often argumentative, resistant to discuss things, resistant to agree even if they know they should or actually do. A closed spirit avoids us, doesn't seek our advice, doesn't respect us, becomes critical of us, and/or shows declining affection or romantic gestures toward us.

Many times we can feel it in their touch or see it in their facial expressions towards us.

Most women can become closed spirits more easily than men because they live in the more sensitive sides of their brains more than men. Women also are usually more sensitive to the non-verbal indicators than men.

So, what can we do to open up a closed spirit? We can ask for forgiveness. We can begin to touch our partner in a mental, non-sexual way.

We can acknowledge that the person seems to be hurting and indicate it was never our intention. We can become more gentle, and tenderhearted.

If, at first, the person does *not* open up, which is not unusual for a woman, then increase your understanding and empathy. Try being even more gentle.

No one said it would be easy. But if the relationship has value to you, it will be worth it in the end.

Open your mouth… just… one… more… time!

Golf Gimme 7:

What are the Odds of an Albatross?

Do you remember the cola commercial where a little boy is out playing golf, and he gets a hole-in-one? He's playing by himself and has no witnesses. He looks all around and sees no one, thinking there's no proof that it even happened.

In the next scene, we see the greens keeper telling him he thinks he owes him a drink of Coke or Pepsi, whichever the advertiser was. For a hole-in-one to be official, you have to have a witness. I think the PGA requires three witnesses.

I was out practicing one day by myself in the afternoon, just like normal in preparation to go out and play a tour event. I had been trying to find a club that I could hit about 230 yards into the wind.

On that particular day, I was carrying my hybrid and a three iron I had bent strong. The wind was up so I brought these clubs out to try.

I came to a par five and crushed a drive. I was sitting dead center in the Fairway about 230 yards to the pin. A perfect opportunity to try these clubs. I dropped two balls and struck one of the clubs.

I knew the green slanted right to left, so I selected a line a little right of the pin. The ball looked perfect, but I could not see it end up on the green, so I assumed that went over the back of the green.

I selected the other club out of my bag, and struck it to about 15 feet pin high, left of the pin.

What Are the Odds of an Albatross?

I drove to the back of the green expecting to see my first ball over the back slightly. I did not see a ball, and I continued to look past the green.

But not far beyond the green over the cart path was the desert. I could not imagine that I'd hit the ball that far, as it would've been close to 280 yards into the wind.

Suddenly, a wild idea came into my head as I walked to putt my second ball. I thought, "What if that ball went into the cup? That would explain why couldn't find it."

I peered over the edge and to my amazement the ball laid near the center against the pin. Like the little boy in the advertisement, I looked all around to see if anyone had witnessed it.

My luck was not as good as the little boy in the commercial. I had accomplished my first 3 under par hole, or what is referred to as a double eagle or *Albatross*, in my life, and I had no witness but me! So, I did what any good golfer would do. I bought myself a Coke!!

Fuzzy Zoeller and John Gehrisch

If you're interested, **statesman.com** said that the odds of a hole-in-one are about 13,000 to 1. I've had a number of hole-in-ones, but only one Albatross so far in my life. The statesman quotes the odds of an Albatross as 6 million-to-1.

To give you an idea, according to them, about 40,000 hole-in-ones happen each year. There are only about 200 albatrosses. They further state that only about 10% of golfers are capable of even reaching a par five in two.

Probably the most famous double eagle was by Gene Sarazen in the 1935 Masters. In the final round, Craig Wood was finishing his round and had a three-stroke lead over Sarazen. Gene stood in the 15th fairway. Sarazen holed out his 4-wood from 235 yards for a two Albatross. He went on to tie Wood and then won in a 36-hole playoff the next day.

Jeff Maggert scored a double eagle on the par-5 13th at Augusta in the 1994 Masters. Then, in the 2001 British Open, he made double eagle on the par-5 sixth hole at Royal Lytham & St. Annes. He is the only golfer to make double eagle in two majors.

T. C. Chen is painfully remembered for his double-hit chip in the final round of the 1985 U.S. Open at Oakland Hills.

But history recorded him making the first double eagle in his first round at the U.S. Open on the 527-yard second hole, dropping a ball to the bottom of the cup with a 3-wood from 256 yards out.

Hole #8

Divorce Eye-Openers

*"Staying married may have long-term benefits.
You can elicit much more sympathy from friends over a bad marriage than
you ever can from a good divorce."*
-- Jake "P. J." O'Rourke (1947 -)
American political satirist

Various studies on the U.S. rate of divorce show significant differences when a comparison is made in 1st, 2nd, and 3rd marriage breakups in America. My research found that the marriage breakup rate in America for a first marriage varies from 41% to 50%. The rate for a second marriage jumps to between 60% and 67%. And the divorce rate in America for 3rd marriage divorces ranges between 73% and 74%. The percentage differences vary depending on whom I have read. No matter which number you use, the percentage of failure is horrible.

Reports also say that couples *with* children have a slightly lower rate of breakup as compared to couples *without* children. This is due to the fact that being childless, when children are wanted, can be one of the prime causes of divorce for such a couple.

Also, the children of divorced parents are prone to divorcing four times more often than the children of couples who are *not* divorced.

We must think seriously about this before divorcing if we have children. We are likely to affect our children's future.

I am not saying that you should stay in a bad marriage for the children's sake. I *am* saying to make sure you have done everything possible before bailing on the marriage.

Really, that should always be the route, with or without children, but it should be mandatory if children are involved, since divorce affects not only the future of the couple, but that of the children, too.

My goal is to greatly reduce these unhappy percentages by arming people so they do not make bad choice mistakes in the first place. These percentage numbers are just plain staggering and unacceptable to me. With this book, I hope to help save troubled marriages.

Breakdowns are usually caused by such things as:
- lack of values,
- poor communication,
- misunderstanding,
- different perceptions of the meaning of commitment,
- lack of loyalty,
- irresponsibility, and
- an unwillingness to work together to sustain the family unit.

Marriage, after all, is the legal, verbal, and moral commitment made between two people. It is the agreement to support, and commit to each other to fulfill their objectives and goals in order to enable each other to contribute to the economic and general welfare of the family unit as a whole.

A family united by love is a family unit that will prosper and endure almost anything. The secret here is to make love last.

Among the main foundation secrets to a *Happy, Loving, Long-Term Relationship* are trust, love, and the constant unity of the couple. This is what holds it all together. But this is only the foundation. You'll see more in my formula later.

But if a troubled marriage has a chance of being saved, perhaps I can help them salvage their relationship if they, and "they" is the primary word here, are willing to work at it.

This will almost always take a serious commitment on both parties to salvage a troubled marriage.

One way we can cause a marriage to fail is to try to dominate our partner. Marrying a controlling person can happen to anyone. The warning signs of a controlling person in a relationship can be intense financial management, where the wife or husband demands total accountability for every dollar spent, assuming, of course, that both people are able to be responsible regarding finances.

Jealousy can also cause domination of a partner. The situations can be different, but recognizing if your wife or husband is behaving in ways that are controlling or abusive, can help you to regain control of your life within that relationship.

If you feel your wife or husband is controlling or abusive, you may want to research and find a well-respected counselor. That said, I must stress that there are many *poor* counselors that will do more harm than good. Be careful to reach out only to a *good* counselor, as a competent one may help to save the marriage or relationship.

I remember going to a counselor during the divorce proceedings of my first marriage. While standing in the waiting room for our appointment, I read an article framed on the wall about the counselor my ex-wife had chosen. I read how the female counselor was an only daughter and had raised herself up from a male-dominated family of a father and eight brothers.

Because of this, I pretty much knew what was coming. I was right.

We walked in for our appointment, sat down and introduced ourselves. The counselor's first question to me was, "Do you think the relationship is salvageable?"

I said, "No." Even though I thought I was prepared, what came next amazed me. She did not ask me why. In fact, she did not ask me any other questions.

She simply said, "Well then, I guess my job is to prepare your wife to meet other men."

I replied, "Really?" Okay, then I stood up and walked out.

The woman actually had the gall to send me a bill.

So, do some serious research to find a good quality counselor. There *are* good ones. And there are some *really* bad ones!! Case in point.

The odds are extremely high that no one will divorce a partner that holds value for a person offering them unconditional love, respect, and support. These are almost certainly what most people want in their marriage.

Longevity, in most marriages, is directly proportional to the work put in together.

Success comes when both people invest to achieve the best in life for them and their family, and by the joint work applied together toward a common goal. Then and *only* then can that marriage become and stay strong.

Do not be a quitter like the majority today. Do not destroy your marriage, rather work on your relationship with your partner. Make the effort needed to rebuild a happy life with your partner.

Leaving and then looking for happiness in the next relationship is the lazy way. It is also likely to have the same types of challenges, and, ultimately, the same results.

Remember, one definition of insanity is doing the same things over and over, but expecting different results. Life does not work that way. If we do the same things over and over, we get the same results. To bring about different results takes commitment from both people in the relationship. That commitment is one of the vital ingredients in the JAG Formula for a *Happy, Loving, Long-Term Relationship*. You will read about this in Hole #15.

You will not have a *Happy, Loving, Long-Term Relationship* if you attempt to control your partner by attempting to brainwash them or by making them believe that they are inferior to you.

You will fail your relationship if you attempt to make them feel they are incapable of achieving their goals.

Actually, if you refuse to allow them to be better than yourself, by having a better job or making more money than you, then you place your leadership in jeopardy. Your decision-making process in your own home becomes suspect.

As men, many times we believe that we *have* to be the ones that earn the most money or have the best-paying career. We each try to be the proverbial "man of the house." In many cases, this undermines the man's ability to be the best husband he can be.

This thinking can stunt his ability to support his mate in happiness, as the world is changing. Women earn more than their spouses at many times. Of course, a woman can only do this when she is supported to do so.

When the man becomes non-supportive of his wife's attempts at success, or he becomes a tyrant in other ways in the relationship, his partner will generally reject him, sooner or later, and file for divorce.

Remember, love is given freely, can be withdrawn at any time, and is not a possession.

You do not own your partner. Love is a gift that is given freely and should be honored. We all need to *give* love and support in order to *receive* love and support in return. We must help our partner to be the best he or her can be.

Interestingly, those who divorce rarely marry the person with whom they are having the affair.

For example, Dr. Jan Halper's study of successful men (executives, entrepreneurs, and professionals) found that very few men who cheat, divorce their wife, and then marry their lovers.

Only three percent of the 4,100 successful men surveyed eventually married their lovers.

It is not just men who will opt for a divorce. According to the Huffington Post, divorce could be in a woman's genes. In February, 2012, Swedish scientists released a study suggesting that a specific gene may explain why some women have a hard time committing or staying committed, should they marry.

The researchers found that women who possessed a variation of the oxytocin receptor gene known as A-allele were less likely to get married due to difficulty bonding with other people. Those with the gene who *did* marry were 50 percent more likely to report "marital crisis."

Interestingly, in November, 2012, a 26-year longitudinal study, released by the University of Michigan, found that when a husband reported having a close relationship with his wife's parents, the couple's risk of divorce *decreased* by 20%.

Strangely, but on the other hand, when a wife reported having a close relationship with her husband's parents, the couple's risk of divorce *increased* 20%. Go figure.

Men, beware!! According to a study released in May, 2012, by the University of Florence, "sudden coital death" is more common when a man is engaging in extramarital sex in an unfamiliar setting than when he's having sex with his spouse at home.

The researchers found that infidelity outside the home was associated with "a higher risk of a major cardiovascular event," including fatal heart attacks.

"Extra-marital sex may be hazardous and stressful because the lover is often younger than the primary partner, and probably sex occurs more often following excessive drinking and/or eating," researcher Dr. Alessandra Fisher told the *Daily Mail*.

"It is possible that a secret sexual encounter in an unfamiliar setting may significantly increase blood pressure and heart rate, leading to increased oxygen demand."

So, stay true to your spouse. If not because you have morals, then do it because your life may depend on it!

A University of Cincinnati study, presented in August, 2012, found that men are more likely to turn to drinking after a divorce. You may recall TC's comments in Hole #2 – "Help for Tin Cup." He spoke of beginning to drink more.

Also, don't ignore those pre-wedding jitters. They may warn of marital trouble ahead. That's according to a UCLA study, published in the Journal of Family Psychology in September, 2012. Researchers asked 232 newlyweds, all in their first marriages, whether they had "ever been uncertain or hesitated about getting married" after they got engaged. The research team followed up with the couples every six months for the first four years of their marriages.

In a Huff Post Blog, one of the researchers, Justin Lavner, explained that premarital doubts predicted divorce rates four years later, especially when the doubtful partner was the wife.

According to Lavner, "19 percent of couples in which wives had doubts were divorced four years later, but only 8 percent of couples in which wives did not have doubts ended up divorced. Husbands' doubts did not significantly predict divorce, although divorce rates were somewhat higher among husbands with doubts (14 percent) than husbands without doubts (9 percent)."

Living together before marriage is no longer a strong predictor of divorce, according to a study released by the Centers for Disease Control and Prevention in early 2012.

As part of a marriage survey of 22,000 men and women, researchers found that those who were engaged and living together before the wedding were about as likely to have marriages that lasted 15 years as couples who hadn't cohabited.

What about couples who moved in together but weren't engaged? The study found their marriages were less likely to survive to the 10- and 15-year marks.

More couples are opting for long-term marital separations because they cannot afford to divorce, according to a study conducted by Ohio State University that was published in August, 2012.

Researchers surveyed 7,272 people between 1979 and 2008. Most people in the study who separated from a spouse reported getting a divorce within three years of separating. But 15% of people who separated did not get a divorce within the first 10 years.

Divorce at a younger age hurts people's health more than divorce later in life, according to a Michigan State University Study released in January, 2012.

Divorce Statistics and Divorce Rate in the USA
(from **divorcestatistic.com**)

According to divorcestatistic.com the rate of divorce in America is high. It has even reported by various organizations that the rate is 50%.

However, this may not be completely true as some data reveals that the figure is lower. Regardless, if current trends continue, soon the figure *will* reach 50% and even more.

When we discuss stats, they should be actual and legitimate, but much depend on many factors. U.S. divorce statistics are also gathered by a number of diverse agencies, such as the U.S. Census Bureau, the Centers for Disease Control and Prevention, the National Center for Health Statistics, and the independent Americans for Divorce Reform. The stats probably are not comprehensive, but the figures help a lot in understanding the meaning of divorce in the highly modern society of America.

So, let's begin with a table of age at marriage.

Age	Women	Men
Under 20 years old	27.6%	11.7%
20 to 24 years old	36.6%	38.8%
25 to 29 years old	16.4%	22.3%
30 to 34 years old	8.5%	11.6%
35 to 39 years old	5.1%	6.5%

Drop in Divorce Rate:

Rates have been dropping during the last few decades. Data indicates that marriages have lasted longer in the 21st century as compared to the success rate of marriages in the 1990s. Also, experts believe that the current rate trend might go down more in coming years, as more and more couples prefer a live-in relationship. This is a type of relationship where couples live together like partners without marrying. But actual married couples may have a higher divorce rate in the future based on some studies.

In 2008, a study was conducted by Jenifer L. Bratter and Rosalind B. King on behalf of the Education Resources Information Center. In this detailed study, the main topic was whether crossing racial boundaries increased the risk of ending a marriage. After detailed study, it has been found that interracial couples have higher rates of divorce, particularly for those that married during the late 1980s.

In interracial divorce cases gender plays a big role. Interracial marriages with highest divorce rate took place between White females and non-White males. White wife/Black husband marriages are also more likely to result in divorce by the 10th year of marriage as compared to White/White couples. Also White wife/Asian husband marriages are more likely to end in divorce as compared to White/White marriages. As you can see, many things factor in to actual divorce rates.

More U.S. Divorce Statistics

Divorce and Marriage rates in the US for 2002
Source: Divorce Magazine, May 23, 2004

Marriage and Divorce Statistics (2002)
Percentage of population that is married: 59%
    (down from 62% in 1990, 72% in 1970)

Percentage of population that has never married: 24%

Percentage of population that is divorced: 10%
    (up from 8% in 1990, 6% in 1980)

Percentage of population that is widowed: 7%

Median age at first marriage: Males: 26.9
    Females: 25.3

Median age at first divorce: Males: 30.5
    Females: 29

Median age at second marriage: Males: 34
    Females: 32

Median age at second divorce: Males: 39.3
    Females: 37

Median duration of first marriages that end in divorce:
Males: 7.8 years
Females: 7.9 years

Median duration of second marriages that end in divorce:
Males: 7.3 years
Females: 6.8 years

Median number of years people wait to remarry after their first divorce:
Males: 3.3 years
Females: 3.1 years

Percentage of married people who reach their 5th, 10th, and 15th anniversaries:
5th: 82%
10th: 65%
15th: 52%

Percentage of married people who reach their 25th, 35th, and 50th anniversaries:
25th: 33%
35th: 20%
50th: 5%

Percentage of people who have ever been married by the age of 25:
Males: 32%
Females: 50%

Percentage of people who have ever been married by the age of 35:
Males: 77%
Females: 84%

Percentage of people who have ever been married by the age of 45:
Males: 87%
Females: 90%

Percentage of people who have ever been married by the age of 55:
Both males and females: 95%

Number of unmarried couples living together: 5.5 million

Percentage of unmarried couples living together that are male-female unions: 89%

<u>Children/Single parents</u>: (2000, except where noted)

Percentage of households which are family households: 68.8%

Percentage of households with their own children under 18: 33%

Percentage of married householders with kids: 24%

Percentage of all households run by single moms: 9.2%

Percentage of all households run by single dads: 1.9%

Number of single parents: Males: 2.04 million
Females: 9.68 million

Percentage of children under 18 years of age living with both parents (2002): 69%

Percentage of children under 18 years of age living with mother only (2002): 23%

Percentage of children under 18 years of age living with father only (2002): 5%

Percentage of children under 18 years of age living with neither parent (2002): 4%

Total single fathers maintaining their own household:
1.786 million

Total single fathers living in the home of a relative: 240,000

Total single fathers who are divorced: 913,000

Total single fathers never married: 693,000

Total single fathers raising one child: 1,300,000

Total single fathers raising four or more children: 55,000

Total single mothers maintaining their own household:
7.571 million

Total single mothers living in the home of a relative: 1.633 million

Total single mothers who are divorced: 3.392 million

Total single mothers never married: 4.181 million

Total single mothers raising one child: 5.239 million

Total single mothers raising four or more children: 475,000

It is important to note that fatherless homes account for 63% of youth suicides, 90% of homeless/ runaway children, 85% of children with behavior problems, 71% of high school dropouts, 85% of youths in prison, and well over 50% of teen mothers.

 Golf Gimme 8:

My First PGA Tournament

A professional acquaintance of mine was the assistant at the Lake Winnipesaukee Golf Club. I was hitting some balls on the practice range prior to teeing it up with some friends when I noticed him walking towards me. He had qualified to play on the Canadian PGA tour the previous year.

As he closed in on me and noticed I was looking up, he said, "Hi John! How are you hitting them?" I replied that I wasn't striking the ball too badly considering some of the physical things I had gone through.

I had experienced a torn meniscus in my knee, which had required surgery. At the same time, I had a torn cartilage in my shoulder and the release of a shredded bicep tendon, which also required surgery. Worst of all, they found a cancer mass.

Fortunately, the cancer was the type that could be cured. The process was long and arduous. Finally, I had gone through all of the chemotherapy they could give me. The mass that had begun the size of a softball between my stomach and hip bone had only been reduced to the size of a golf ball.

So, I then went through radiation five days a week for five weeks. Fortunately, the cancer was gone, but after the surgeries and cancer, my professional golf days were behind me. I never was quite the same again. Striking the ball well that day was pleasing, as I did not play or practice much anymore.

He next said to me, "You did not warn me. There's a lot more to playing the tour than just being able to hit a golf ball well!"

I said, "Yes! You're correct. You did not ask!"

We both laughed.

I said, "You have to be your own travel agent. You have to adjust to different time zones and sometimes different cultures in different countries. You find yourself adjusting to different golf courses every week.

"If you're playing the Monday qualifiers, and get into a tournament, you have to leave late Sunday after competing, travel to the next destination, and be ready to play first thing Monday morning on a golf course you've likely never seen before.

"Then there is playing the Pro-Am's during the week of the tournament, playing with players with every different handicap and personality imaginable. It's not like playing social golf where you can choose your playing partners. You take the luck of the draw on that when you are on tour.

"You have to learn to deal with your personal demons out there also, getting them and keeping them in check and not putting unnecessary pressure on yourself. There are many other things that I'm sure you have discovered. One of the larger ones for most competitors is the pressure of knowing you have to win enough money to cover your expenses to stay out there, especially if you don't have a sponsor. I was lucky because I was self-funded, so I didn't have to worry about that. But most players do. Also, if you don't win enough money for the year or the all-time money list, you can lose your players card. I'm sure you can relate to all of this."

He said, "Boy that's for sure!"

He asked me what my first tournament was like. I had to laugh a little thinking back on it.

I told him how it all started with one of my best male friends in the world, Butch Baird. Butch eventually played the tour for 42 years, and he was kind enough to take me under his wing.

My first Champions tour tournament was the Master Card Mexican Open in Mexico. Butch and I were discussing the upcoming tournament. Butch asked me what I was going to eat while I was there.

I said, "Well, I was thinking about a lot of salads and vegetables."

He said, "No! No! Salads are *warshed* in the water."

Butch was originally from Texas and Chicago and pronounced the word *wash,* as *warsh.* I was from Ohio and said it the same way. I was one of the few people that understood him when he talked about *warshing* things.

"I had not thought of that, Butch," I said. "I knew I did not want to drink the water, but I didn't think about foods being *warshed* in it, too."

As it turned out, the resort the PGA had set us up in, had treated water, so we were going to be ok after all. But we did not know that before leaving. It needed to be considered.

Then Butch had said, "Don't forget your painter's mask."

Butch is a prankster just as I am. I think maybe that's part of the reason that he and I are such great friends.

I said, "Painter's mask?"

I thought for a moment, trying to figure out where this joke was headed. I was coming up blank.

"Okay, Butch, I'll bite," I said. "Why do I need to take a painter's mask?"

He knew I thought he was joking with me and said, "Dammit, John, I told you I will never kid you about golf! Golf is our livelihood. Go buy some painter's masks!"

I questioned, "WHY?"

He said, "The volcano is erupting down there right now. If the ash gets in the air while we are playing, you will not be able to breath! Now go down to Home Depot and buy some painter's masks!"

So, I reluctantly did.

When I arrived in Mexico, I was greeted at the airport by a driver from the PGA to shuttle me to the resort where we were staying. I still was wondering in my mind if Butch was playing a joke on the rookie as we drove along in the countryside. This was a pretty remote area. I even saw wild dogs running loose.

I did not know there would be police, and I mean armed men with machine guns, standing guard outside the course when I arrived the next day!

As we drove along, I looked out the passenger side window. Suddenly, I saw a mountain protruding from the distant landscape. To my surprise, smoke bellowed out of the top of that mountain.

My dear friend really would not kid me about golf. He'd been looking after the rookie, not playing a joke on me at all. Most other tournament players there would not have told me that! After all, I was a competitor. Anything they can do to get one up on you can mean money in their pocket. I was on my own, except for my good friend's help.

I was able to play a practice round. Then I drew an early tee time on the morning of the tournament, so I would be one of the first to start that day.

I have a ritual that I developed that is very consistent. I discovered that consistency is important out there.
- I would always arrive at the course an hour and a half early, minimum.
- I would do my formal check-in.
- I would touch base with Titlist and get some golf balls.

- I would find out who my caddy was, since I normally elected not to bring one.
- I would go to the putting green and practice putting for 30 minutes.
- I would test my caddy out to see if he could read greens well enough for me to ask his opinion occasionally or not.

In this case, I discovered that he could not speak English, and he could not read a green at all. I had put in for a bag carrier, not a real caddy. That's what happens to Rookies not experienced enough to make better arrangements.

Normally, I found reading my own putts was a better way to go for me anyway. Unless somebody knows you really well, they do not typically know the speed at which the ball will arrive at the cup for you.

If a player is aggressive, the break will be less on the green. If he tends to lie the ball in the cup, the break will be more noticeable, and you have to adjust for that. Unless a Caddy works with you every day, it is hard for them to know your putting style consistently and read greens to help you to a high degree of efficiency.

I also found that if I envisioned the putt in my mind's eye, I made a higher percentage.

Next, I would go to the practice tee. For tournaments, I would warm up for 60 minutes, beginning with a pitching wedge, then eight iron, then six iron, then fairway wood, and finishing with a driver. If it was just a practice day, I would alternate to spread the wear on the golf clubs, starting with my nine iron, seven iron, five iron, fairway wood, and then driver. Then I would go to the first tee for check in.

For me and most other players, it's really important that we do not feel rushed in our warm-ups. That can speed up your tempo, and I never wanted that.

The PGA would have a representative to look into your bag and take an inventory of what brand clubs you were playing for each club and putter. They keep those kind of statistics every year. It also is a way for your clubs' sponsor to verify that you *are* playing their clubs.

To this day I am a Tour Staff Member with Ping. I was required to play 11 Ping clubs out of 14. I could vary from playing all Ping, if I chose to. Sometimes I did, and sometimes I did not.

John Gehrisch with PING clubs

My clubs' shafts were all frequency-matched to ± one cycle. To give you an idea, what you buy from your local pro or a golf store can vary by as much as ± 30 cycles (potentially a 60-cycle spread) and still be acceptable.

At least that is the way it used to be. Consistency for us is critical, as I said. In all areas.

Like most tour professionals, I played all metal shafts in my irons and graphite shafts in my woods.

Back then, the graphite shafts were a little inconsistent. You could have a ball jump occasionally, and go an extra 5 or 10 yards. That could make you hit the ball over the green for a back pin placement.

I'm starting to see a few professionals beginning to play graphite shafts in their irons now because they have gotten so much better.

Graphite shafts are softer hitting and easier on your joints. Most amateurs would be better playing graphite now for longevity of their joints. Usually amateurs have enough inconsistency in their swing and smash factor (or strikes in the club face sweet spot), so it does not matter much.

What little difference, if any, there is now in graphite shaft consistency is probably not worth the damage human joints could sustain over time from off-center hits using iron shafts, especially for higher handicappers.

John Gehrisch, sporting Ping hat

Anyway, I explained to my former Canadian Tour friend how I had gone through my putting warm-up and had walked to the practice tee. Normally, I select a spot on the left side, which I learned from Butch will help promote a draw for the day, or I will go somewhere between there and the center of the driving range, depending on where the open stalls were.

I was a few minutes behind in my normal schedule, and I elected to warm up on the right side because it was closer and took less time to walk to it and back again. We had not yet been assigned our golf carts.

You see, on the Champions Tour at that time, we could play out of a golf cart. The rule was that the player could ride in the cart, but the caddy must carry the clubs separately and walk if the pro was riding. If the player elected to walk for any time at all, the caddy could put the clubs in the cart and ride.

The purpose of that was so that the spectators, or gallery, who are trying to follow you, could keep up. They would have a hard time keeping up with carts only. But if one or both of you were walking, then spectators could walk at the same pace.

As usual, I was very focused while striking balls on the practice tee. For some reason I suddenly realized there were a number of other balls flying out on the range along with mine.

On this day, these people were hitting behind me because I was on the right, and I had my back to the rest of the range. I turned around to see who else was hitting balls with me. As I look down the line of competitors, what I saw took me back.

Hitting balls behind me were all these guys I had idolized on television for years. Suddenly, I was out on the range warming up to go compete with these legends. I have to admit I will never forget the thought that went through my mind.

I said to myself, "WHAT THE F!@#$%^&* ARE YOU DOING HERE WITH THESE GUYS?!!?"

A big lump rose in my throat! I started to feel some nervousness as I felt very out of place. After all, many of these guys were playing professionally when I was just a young man, merely thinking of trying the game. The experience they had over me was mind boggling. It had not hit me to that extent like it did at that moment.

Then I started to look at them as individuals. There was one a guy I had bested in a Pro-Am in which we both had played. There was another guy I had beaten in a mini-tour event that he had played in to get his competitive juices flowing before the tour started. I knew that I had beaten Butch at times.

"I *can* play with these guys," I said to myself. "Let's do this!"

I went back to my normal warm-up, put them completely out of my mind, and focused on the task at hand.

I mentioned that Tour Professionals have to deal with their demons. Mine became apparent to me on about the sixth or seventh hole when I hit a bad shot. I found the ball and was able to play it. But the bad shot was in a horrible lie and position. I decided to play it, and hit *another* bad shot!

"Oh, my God! These guys think I don't belong here!"

My demon surfaced, placing more pressure on me and making me hit yet another bad shot. By the time I walked off that hole, I had scored a double bogey without even losing a ball.

I went two over par on one hole. That was rare for me. I was used to breaking par every time I played.

On the next tee, again I said to myself, "These guys think I don't belong here!"

It took me a couple holes to recover my composure. Over time, I realized those guys were so focused on their game, they hardly even knew what I was doing. And they really could not care less!

I needed to focus on my own game, and block them out completely! It was a valuable lesson.

Gradually, I began to rid myself of my demon. But it surfaced again almost a year later when I tried to qualify for the US Senior Open. I had two bad holes, and I took myself out mentally.

I really was shocked when I thought back on it later that day. I knew better and was disappointed in myself to have allowed it to happen.

I recalled playing an amateur event years earlier. I had had a bad hole, but I told myself it was a tough golf course, and everyone would have a bad hole. On that day I tied for second because I stayed tough and played each hole on its own.

Sometimes, what we learn in golf, as in life, has to be revisited to remind ourselves of what the resolution to the problem is, even though we had discovered it years before.

I shared my story with the local pro who had played the Canadian Tour for one year, but was unable to repeat the next.

He said he could really relate. He wished he had talked more to me before he tried it on tour.

Who knows, maybe he could have been playing the next year if we had talked. We will never know. Life is funny that way sometimes.

Hole #9

Warning Signs of a Taker Personality

*"Love is spending the rest of your life with someone you want to kill,
but not doing it because you'd miss them."*

-- Unknown

I spoke of the importance of avoiding a "Taker" personality when choosing a partner for a great relationship. Sometimes, however, it can be difficult to recognize a "Taker" personality, especially early in a relationship. Here are some warning signs that can help you avoid the pain by picking up early on signals.

1. They act entitled to whatever they're taking from you.

2. They treat you as an extension of themselves, rather than an independent individual.

3. When they disappoint or hurt you, they don't experience guilt, shame, or remorse.

4. They won't apologize to you, but they do expect you to apologize to them.

5. Their wish is your command, but if you don't comply, you don't love them.

6. They believe their problems are always someone else's fault.

7. They believe that you and everyone else are in this world to make them happy.

8. When you give to them, they don't feel compelled to say thank you or be grateful.

9. If they feel taken from by you, they become outraged and entitled to become enraged.

10. They don't regret taking from you, but they regret not taking even more from you.

11. They need to have the last word in conversations.

12. They are almost never happy or satisfied. (They will want two dresses if you offer to buy them one. If you buy them two dresses, they will want three. Buy them 7 dresses, they will want matching shoes!)

13. They are impatient and hate to wait.

14. They interrupt or butt into conversations.

15. They act as if they are always right.

16. They act as if they are never wrong.

17. When they're frustrated, they feel justified in doing anything to make themselves feel better.

18. They won't tell you specifically what you are doing wrong or ask you directly for what they need. They expect you to read their minds.

19. They are stubborn, and you may confuse their stubbornness with strength and be attracted to them because of it.

20. They aren't motivated to know, care, or do anything unless it gets them something.

21. They are quick to ridicule or laugh at others, but they have little ability to laugh at themselves. Nor can they tolerate being laughed at.

22. They do things they want to do, without taking into account how it affects others.

23. They hold everyone else accountable, but they evade being held accountable.

24. They talk much more than they listen.

25. They'll expect a second, third, and fourth chance from you when they hurt you. However, if they feel hurt *by* you, they won't give you a second chance.

26. They are almost never happy for long.

27. You may never be enough for them. They may want others, too.

Golf Gimme 9:

A Pain in the Neck

Butch Baird, a PGA Tour player with fifteen wins, Shelley Hamlin, LPGA Champion with 5 wins, and Bill Johnston (now in his 90's), a two-time PGA Tour Champion with 45 lifetime wins, and myself used to play a self-determined tournament called the Pine Cone Classic. It's so named because of all the pinecone pranks Butch and I have played on each other.

We even have a pinecone trophy that the loser gets to take home and must display prominently. The trophy of shame, so to speak.

John pointing to Pine Cone Classic trophy, with Bill Johnston

Butch and I were teamed against Shelley and Bill. Typically, Shelley and Bill will play from the white tees, and Butch and I will play back. Fortunately, Butch and I have somehow repeatedly avoided the trophy against these great PGA Champions!

About 10 years ago, when Bill Johnston could still break par routinely on the 6300-yard golf course, we had one of our matches on a golf course called Chihuahua, at the Desert Mountain Golf Club, where I was a member.

At the end of nine holes, Shelley and Bill had Butch and me down by six holes. Butch and I thought that this might be the day we reluctantly accepted the trophy.

On the par 3 Hole #12, Butch and I had the honors and had already hit our tee shots. Shelley had just hit her shot onto the green. Butch and I were standing about 15 feet behind her. Loud enough so that Shelley and Bill could hear, Butch said, "I'm not sure I can finish this match! I have pulled something in my neck."

Standing beside Butch I asked, "Butch, is your neck getting stiff really quickly?"

He confirmed that it was.

I said, "I know what's wrong, and I can fix it."

Butch replied, "I don't think I want you messing with my neck!"

I then replied, "Dammit, Butch. I know what I'm doing! Let me help you."

I placed my right hand on the back of his neck right where it connects to his shoulders. I took hold of his chin with my left hand. I then told him, "This will hurt for an instant, and then all the pain will go away. Your neck will be free again."

Butch's face showed obvious concern and lack of trust.

"Butch, I'm going to count to three, and then I will pull your chin towards me. Just relax as much as possible," I coached.

Butch replied, "Are you sure about this?"

"Yes," I said firmly.

Bill and Shelley watched intently as I began to count. "One, two, three."

As I said the word three out loud, I pulled Butch's chin toward me, and there was a horrible crunch sound!

Shelley screamed!

To ease her discomfort, we pulled the empty water bottle from the back of Butch's shirt where my hand had crunched it at the same time as I had pulled his chin. Shelley was relieved when she realized it was all just a joke.

"Dammit, John," she said in disgust. "I knew you didn't know what you were doing!!!"

At this point you might be thinking that Butch and I will do almost anything to not lose a match. When it comes to the Pine Cone Classic, you would be right!! LOL. And it must have worked.

This day turned out to be one of the most amazing I've ever experienced on a golf course. At the end of 18 holes, Butch and I had not only become even in the match with Shelley and Bill, we had closed them out, making them the losers.

What an incredible comeback!

What was more impressive is that the day had yielded 24 birdies between the four of us. Bill had five, Shelley had six, Butch had six, and I had seven. I had never before seen so many birdies in the foursome.

More importantly, Shelley and Bill took home the trophy… again!!

LOL

Left to right: Butch Baird, Bill Johnston, Shelley Hemlin, John Gehrisch

Here are a couple of delightful relationship tidbits. 2016 marked the 16th wedding anniversary for Butch and Pam Baird. Even more wonderful? On September 3, 2016, Bill Johnston and his wife, JoAnne, celebrated 63 years of marriage.

Congratulations, dear friends!

Snack Shack

A Dear John Letter Worth Sharing

"I believe that love can begin with a smile. A touch can be the fertilizer that makes love begin to grow. A kiss can help it bloom into a relationship. Making wonderful love can begin to build the foundation of the couple as a family unit. Looks can deceive and fade away. The inner beauty is critical. Wealth can be lost. Discovering someone who makes you smile is crucial because it only takes a smile to make a dark day seem bright. So, find the person who makes your heart smile, a best friend in whom there is something that makes you miss them every moment when they are away from you. Find the person who can almost read your mind and somehow instinctively knows your needs, moods, weaknesses, turn-ons, and the depths of your heart, while being trustworthy, responsible, caring, and selfless. Then you have found true love, my friend."

-- John A. Gehrisch
American Entrepreneur and Tour Golf Professional

Date: Oct 8, 2015 GMT

Dear John,

Dear, you mentioned that you have developed a formula for a *Happy, Loving, Long-Term Relationships*. After speaking with you, I am excited and look forward to your book. And did you think about how we fall in love and about how we understand if a person is that one and only?

How do you know when you love someone? You find yourself thinking about them, not just the way they look, and what it feels like to have them close to you, but about their life, what drives them, what concerns them, and what they want. You want to know them and really understand them.

You care about how they spend their time and what's on their mind. You are physically attracted to them and want to be near them.

You like looking at them and want to touch them. You want good things to happen for this person, and you think about what you can do for them to help make their life or maybe just their day better.

It hurts you to see this person in pain. When making decisions that will affect both of you, you naturally place this person's needs above or at least at an equal level to your own. As you get to know the person, and you learn about some of their faults, you accept them as part of the whole person. When you don't see or talk to this person for a while, you miss them, but you understand that this person has a life of their own.

Is that how you see this, John? Or do you think when people get older, that is more about consideration than about emotions?

Hug you,

Inessa

Hole #10

A Few Things Every Man Needs

"You meet someone and you're sure you were lovers in a past life. After two weeks with them, you realize why you haven't kept in touch for the last two thousand years."

-- Al Cleathen
As quoted in "Men Are Slobs; Women Are Neat"

Although I have covered why I think women should look for right-brained men, I will share how you might be able to salvage the left-brained relationship, if you are willing. But the following is important for even the right-brained man. Remember, even right-brained men can be partially left-brained at times. So, if you want his unrivaled devotion let me share some secrets.

The left-brained tendency can provide an important contribution to a relationship.

Why? When the man's competitive part, which comes from the left brain, is guided toward attaining a successful relationship, it can cause huge growth within it. Once he identifies his goal or target, and he sees it is reachable, his conquering nature takes over. The decision-making characteristic of the left brain also assists in providing a foundation, as a structure for the relationship. As the man identifies the benefits of the decision, the commitment becomes much clearer as the obvious "right choice." This makes it easier for him, regardless of his other feelings.

Therefore, he will make the decision to spend time doing something like having a meaningful discussion with his partner, even though he really would rather avoid it. So, why is this a critical thing for a partnership? That one's easy.

If you look at the true basis for love, it is not just a feeling, but rather a decision.

How can a woman place a value on the way her mate thinks, appreciates, and reflects on things? There are a number of ways.

One of the most important things is the man must feel appreciated and admired by others. This becomes especially critical from the woman in his life. Most men will do almost anything to get and receive it. If they do not get it at home, they will literally seek it elsewhere. I have seen it where couples have been married for years, and suddenly the man is lured away by some younger girl who is impressed with his success and shows him admiration. He may love his wife, but over the years she has begun to take for granted all he does to support his family. He misses being openly admired by her and his family. As part of his nature, he needs the gratification of appreciation.

Suddenly, he finds it elsewhere. Whether he seeks it out or finds it by accident, he needs it. He craves it. He almost cannot exist happily without it. And the new woman, excited by all he does, steals his heart away.

No man makes perfect decisions all of the time. Personally, I have never cheated in a committed relationship, even when I did not feel appreciated. But I *will* tell you that I longed for that appreciation. When I got it from others, I could understand where weaker men could be swayed. I cannot judge them for it. Most days I got up through the motivation of doing for my family. I noticed a real slow downturn in motivation during my divorced days. Only when I saw a potential admiring woman in my life, did I feel revitalized.

Ladies, make sure that the person who is showing your man admiration and appreciation is *you*, and *not* some other woman. Finding even simple ways to express your genuine admiration and appreciation will benefit the relationship in huge ways. Please believe me when I say that you both will be the benefactors.

By the way, the key word in the previous sentence is *"genuine."* A man will ultimately see right through fake compliments.

Acknowledge anything he does well and be sincere. You will find there are many things if you just look for them. I think you will find things he does every day that you overlook in everyday life.

"Thank you, Honey." I really appreciate that you take out the garbage every week for me without my asking."

"You are such a good husband."

Simple things work wonders.

Consider this for perspective. Who will be doing all these things if you get divorced, and he is no longer around doing these thing for you and the family. But, rather, he *is* doing all those things for that cute secretary who gave him appreciation when you did not?

Truly, sometimes the simplest of things can make the biggest differences.

The second thing that I suggest is to spend time with him doing things "he" enjoys doing. Usually these involve some sport or recreational thing. Playing a sport, going to a game, or going camping maybe as examples.

Ask yourself, "What is his passion?" Then, take part.

This is one thing that can help retain his interest in you and help you to become or remain best friends. Certainly, sometimes we all like to spend time with our peers or fellow same sex friends. But you may find that you can actually really enjoy it, and you'll begin to take part more and more.

I am not suggesting you have to take up killing animals if hunting is his thing and not yours. What I am saying is to find something you can both enjoy doing together.

Was there something you did together before you were married that you no longer do now that you are married? How well do you know him? You must know his passion! If not, shame on you. Find out immediately!

Now, if you are a guy reading this, you can also do things that your wife loves once in a while, too. A relationship is a two-way street. We are looking to find things that form relationship bonds.

Celebrated author Cathy Burnham Martin goes into this in her book *The Bimbo Has Brains*. In fact, her "take" is that *women* have the very *same* need for appreciation and respect as *men* do. She also expounds on sharing and supporting each other's passions. For example, her husband loves boating. So, she chose to become his First Mate and what she calls his gleeful Galley Girl. She learned to love and look forward to spending time together enjoying his passion.

Thirdly, if you are married, and especially if you have kids, be sure and allocate at least one night to each other per week as "Date Night." This is time just for you and your mate to get away from the kids and keep your relationship alive.

You fell in love for a reason. Don't lose that. When we fall in love, it is supposed to only be the foundation on which we build a tall building that becomes our lifetime relationship.

If you choose wisely, and I am giving you the Secret Formula in this book of items that are key to your success, you can build a gigantic skyscraper that no storm can ever destroy.

Fourth, a man needs is to feel that his advice has value to you. If you roll your eyes when he begins talking to you instead of giving him your full attention, he will feel you consider that his advice holds no value for you.

If you always try to have the last word instead of thanking him for sharing his feelings or thoughts, he will also feel you do not value his advice.

If you pick up your book or page through a magazine while he is talking, instead of setting everything aside while he speaks to you, he will feel you do not value his advice.

If you take exception or criticize him before he is even finished, rather than acknowledging the positive points he mentioned, he will feel you do not value his advice.

Have you ever done this in your relationships ladies?

Men, have you done any of these things to your lady?

These are basic courtesy rules that should be applied in our communications. Remember, when we communicate, non-verbal communication skills are among our most powerful techniques.

The use of eye contact, facial expressions, voice tone, showing sincere interest in what is being said, and exhibiting patience to hear the full thought of the other person before offering meaningful answers or comments is critical to non-verbal skills.

Again, the companion book to this one, *The Bimbo Has Brains*, has a wonderful chapter dealing with details of verbal and nonverbal communications.

Listen. Engage brain before engaging mouth.

LOL

 **Golf Gimme 10:**

Learning to Concentrate

I consider myself really lucky to have become very close friends with Tour Star Butch Baird. He played the Tour for 42 straight years, and he still plays the Legends Tournament.

When I met Butch in the mid 90's, he was tenth on the all-time money winner list. Because the winnings were being raised so dramatically for each tournament, he quickly plummeted over the next few years. That then made it difficult for him to qualify to play in tournaments, eventually forcing him into retirement.

One of the ways in which you can qualify to play in tournaments is the All Time Money List. I really feel the way it's done is unfair. They only look at money won.

I think there should be a point system based on what place you finished in tournaments. For example, arguably the greatest golfer ever, Jack Nicklaus, only won something like $4.9 million in his entire career. Rory McIlroy recently made $11.53 million dollars in one week, when he won the FedEx cup and the Tour Championship tournament.

Butch never allowed anyone to practice with him, but one day he asked me to go for some reason. After warming up, we ventured to the first tee. We both hit two tee balls and selected the worst of the two drives. We then each hit two iron shots to the green and went to the green and putted out our own balls. We went to the next hole and hit two drives again selecting the worst. I was standing watching Butch getting ready to hit.

He looked up at me and said, "Go ahead. Hit!"

I knew I had been invited into a very private and special place. I knew that I had an opportunity to observe and learn from one of the world's greatest players ever. I did not want to bother him or do anything that might cause him to not invite me another time.

I said, "Butch, I don't want to bother you."

Butch backed away from his ball and said, "John, I learned with guys that could do anything, except they would not touch the player or his equipment. I can only concentrate on one thing at a time. If I'm concentrating on what *you're* doing, I cannot concentrate on what *I'm* doing. I won't even know you're hitting!"

So, I went ahead and hit my two balls at the same time he was hitting. We got to the green, and the same thing happened regarding putting. We'd begun to practice every day together, and I was able to pick Butch's brains and learn amazing things.

But the thing that Butch did for me that day and every day after is something that I don't think he even realized. He forced me to concentrate and block out what he was doing. The genius of this man was beginning to become even more apparent to me. The extent to which he would help me was only starting to surface.

I learned a level of concentration that I did not even know existed, even as a good amateur.

After a while, nothing bothered me on the golf course. I would be playing Pro-Ams, for example, and I remember an amateur hitting the accelerator pedal on his golf cart. This kicks the brake pedal off, making a loud noise. It happened right in the middle of my golf swing during the tournament. The amateur was so embarrassed when he realized what he'd done. He apologized profusely.

I said, "For what?"

He told me what he had done.

I said, "I didn't even hear it."

Then, as I walked up the fairway thinking about it, I realize that I had heard it subconsciously, but not consciously. I had learned to block such things out.

The only thing that ever bothered me on the golf course was if I was looking down the line of my putt, and a Marshall moved across in my line of sight left to right, for example.

Invariably, in my mind, I would see enough of that to make the cup move with him. In other words, my target would move to the right with him, and I would miss the putt on the right side. I learned that on the rare occasions when something like that would happen, I needed to stop and start over.

John Gehrisch hitting balls on the range at Augusta
with Colin Montgomery

At one mini tour event, I was over the ball and ready to hit my driver. I took the club back and accelerated downward towards the ball, stopping the club only about a foot away.

I stood up and started my pre-shot routine again and then struck the ball in the middle of the Fairway. As we walked off the tee one of the guys commented, "John, I can't believe you stopped your swing that late."

I said, "Honestly, I can't either."

But I knew I was wrong coming down, and I had that kind of concentration to stop things before it became a disaster. One bad shot in a round, especially in a one-day tournament, can be extremely costly. Sometimes it can make a difference of thousands of dollars, or even making the cut in some tournaments.

As an amateur, I had no idea the concentration level required to play the game at the professional level. It's why people who are in the gallery need to understand that the professionals probably are not going to communicate much with them during a tournament.

Practice rounds? Sure, many will. I heard Butch explain that one day to a man who asked why the pros did not talk more during tournaments.

His explanation was this, "We don't come into your boardroom meetings and interrupt you while you're thinking, strategizing, and working. We simply ask the same courtesy."

You see, as professionals, we try to get every possible advantage we can in our corner. To illustrate this, I remember something that happened when I was playing a tour event. We were standing on the tee of the par three hole, waiting for the group ahead to clear the green.

Someone in the gallery asked if they could ask us a question while we were waiting.

We said, "Sure."

He said, "As good as you professionals are at hitting the ball off the ground, why do you bother to put it on a tee on a par three when you're going to hit an iron?"

One of the other players answered before I could, and actually gave a better answer than I would have.

His answer was, "Because we are playing for a lot of money!"

That really says it all. If it will help you score better, *do it!*

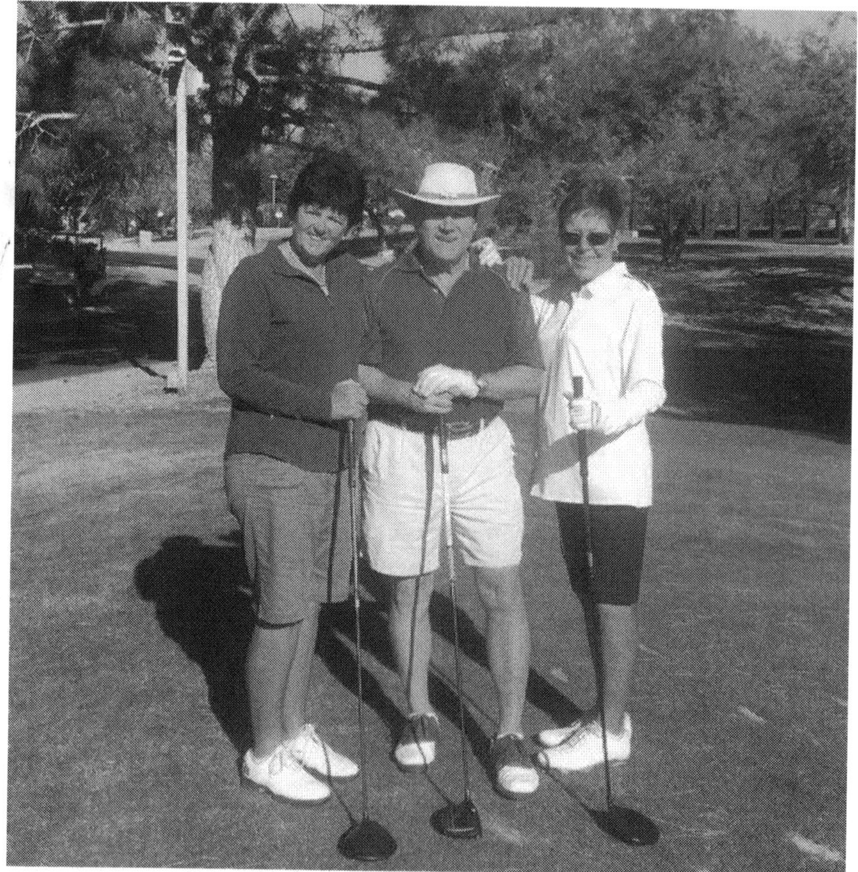

John flanked by two LPGA Champions,
Left to right: Anne-Marie Palli, John Gehrisch, and Shelley Hamlin

Hole #11

The Excitement Factor

"You have to walk carefully in the beginning of love;
the running across fields into your lover's arms can only come later
when you're sure they won't laugh if you trip."

- Jonathan Carroll (1949 -)
American novelist

What may surprise many people here is that women lose the desire for monogamy much faster than men do in a relationship. Unlike a man, their desire plummets off a cliff. And when it goes, it goes fast.

People tend to think that it is a loss of desire for sex and is caused by a chemical change in a woman's body at a certain age. While at times it can be a chemical change within her body, many times it actually is the loss of what I call the "Excitement Factor."

Men lose their desire for monogamy gradually. They can and many times do just say, "Hey babe, are you in the mood for sex?" And they expect their significant other to be ready for action.

The thing that makes most women fall in love and be attracted sexually to her man early in the relationship is the seduction process that builds up the "Excitement Factor." Over time, a man lets that become mundane since he knows she is a sure thing, so to speak. Or because they live together instead of meeting for dates, etc.

Instead of romancing her through the day and/or evening, pacing things, and being playful during the seduction of her, we men let our daily lives get in the way and just expect her to be at our beck and call whenever we want sex. We expect her to be, all ready, primed for action.

Some women can do that. Others may do it out of commitment to the relationship. However, most will not stay in it emotionally and will begin to wander over time. The wandering may be mentally or physically, or both.

Also, women's desire for intimacy can be affected hugely by what is happening in her life at the moment. I mentioned that when a woman has an argument with her mate, she is not likely going to be in the mood to jump his bones.

Another example where her desire will reduce greatly is if she has become insecure about herself, her job, or the relationship. Other things can affect her desire levels as well. She can improve a lack of desire situation by asking herself some questions about her activities that may actually turn herself "off" to intimacy. For example, is it when I do emails? Read certain types of books? Watch TV? Talk with my parents on the phone? Deal with the children doing homework?

If she becomes aware and avoids these things before typical times of intimacy, it can improve things. She can also ask herself, "When do I turn myself on to *wanting* intimacy?" For example, maybe she will find it is on days when she rides her horse, spends time in nature, or plays a certain sport. These things usually makes us feel more secure and good about ourselves.

No matter, the key take-away here is that we men need to try to do little things to keep things exciting for that person who is the love of our life. This keeps her emotionally wanting intimacy and monogamy.

I suggest trying small seductive things periodically. Little seductive notes during the day, for example. Flowers delivered at work or home for no reason. Her favorite candy showing up with a note of appreciation somewhere she would not expect it.

Men ask yourself, "What can I do today to make a difference, even in a small way?"

Always remember that monogamy is not natural. It is a choice, a state of mind, and a willing commitment that can be lost. Both people should remember that all good things should not be taken for granted. It requires some work to keep it alive, therefore keeping the "Excitement Factor" flourishing and healthy. As long as it is healthy, the relationship will typically follow.

Just ahead, in Hole 16, you will find "Discussion Questions to Improve Your Relationship." I think you'll find good ideas to evaluate your relationship in order to improve it.

Meanwhile, the next time you are in a restaurant for lunch where there are business people, notice how nicely they are dressed. They knock themselves out to dress to the nines to impress their bosses and co-workers, usually within their budget, of course. We all put ourselves out there for our job because it is so important to us.

Then we go home and our significant other gets the leftovers. Think about that. We get so comfortable with the most important person in our life that they become unimportant enough to get what's left over. Yet, we expect them to love us anyway.

Ask yourself what is wrong with this picture? I imagine if you are in a lengthy relationship you know about this.

If so, then ask yourself, "What could I do to make this situation better in my own life?" If you are not yet, be aware to keep this from happening because it is so easy to fall into this habit.

In a relationship, we should always be reviewing where we are, and what we can do better. Have you ever had a job where your boss did *not* review your performance and discuss with you what you could do better? This is typically done annually.

Why do most people *not* do this in a relationship, when it is more important than any job?

I will tell you why. Because jobs usually have incentives that are made obvious. This could include a bonus, a commission, or a wage increase associated with improved performance.

In our lives, things change over the years. We change personally. Things change between us as couples. Many times, our relationship needs to be reinvented over time. We might have things happen such as moving or losing of a parent or even a child.

Annually, we should sit down and review our relationships. We should verbalize how our mates can make things better *and* how we think *we* can make things better. This needs to be done with love and an open mind, for the good of the relationship and the happiness of the person we love. Our happiness almost always follows as a by-product.

Recently, I heard a woman speaking about having gone to several couples' retreats. She said that, at first, her husband did not want to go. Yet, afterwards he said he really enjoyed it as much as she did. She said she'd heard another man say the exact same thing her husband had been trying to tell her, but because it came from someone *else*, and because he used different wording, she had a much better understanding about her husband's point of view.

Being able to talk with other women going through similar relationship issues was very soothing as it helped her recognize that she and her husband were not alone in it. This also gave her some helpful, new ideas.

Personally, I have never done this, so I have no direct experience. Still, I find it intriguing. Wives of busy executives shared stories of feeling alone so much because of their husbands' travels, for example.

A good relationship can take some work. Over time, we transform somewhat into the person our significant other wants us to be.

I don't mean that we should change and become someone we are not. And I don't mean we should try to change our mate. I just mean we will naturally pick up certain things that make us even more the person they love.

A good relationship is a "state of being in" either willfully or wantonly. Many times, people feel a commitment is a loss of something, like freedom for example. It should be seen and treated as a natural and desired commitment, without negative connotations or denotative attachments.

You can share your ideas for building a stronger, more loving relationship on my website:

www.GolfProHasHeart.com

Who says that men cannot decorate?

Golf Gimme 11:

All Work and No Play Makes John a Dull Boy

I believe people should work hard, but we should also play hard.

I don't remember anyone ever calling me a dull person. Because I was born on April 1st, I guess I was cursed at birth to be a prankster. Plus I have found that my family, going back many generations, were also pranksters.

 I will share one story about my family. I heard it at my aunt's funeral. Honestly, I didn't believe it first.

This is something that even I probably would not have done. And that's going a ways. LOL

Typically, my family will go to a funeral when someone has passed away, pay our respects, and then go somewhere, as a family, where there is food prepared. There we try to get by the sadness of losing the person.

We basically begin to celebrate the life of the person who died. We begin to tell stories about the person, and typically alcohol appears on the scene. I can't remember ever seeing anyone in my family intoxicated, but they do have a good time and joke a lot.

The story that I heard went like this. My great-grandfather on my grandmother's side had passed away. He owned a farm in Ohio.

Back then, many times they held the funeral in the house, as was the case in this situation. My great-grandfather was laid out in his casket in his "Sunday best," as they used to say.

The family began to drink and tell stories and laugh and recall and rejoice about his life. I never knew my great-grandfather, but I guess he liked to have a lot of fun.

On this particular occasion, the family decided that my great-grandfather was not having a good enough time, so they actually pulled him out of the casket, brought him into the room where everyone was, and propped him up in the corner so he could be part of the group.

When I heard this story, I asked my father if this really happened.

He said, "Oh yes, it happened, and your great-grandfather would've loved it!"

Some of my favorite times in my life have been spent on the golf course, or with people I've met through golf. Tour Star Butch Baird is a perfect example of that. I've had more laughs on the golf course with Butch, than anyone else.

But in fairness, I probably played more with Butch than anyone else because we also practiced together a lot. The stories I could share could be a book of its own. Here's a sample.

First of all, Butch is the guy who started the big hat on tour. He got me wearing one also because it provided better sun protection.

When you spend as much time as we do in the sun, you want to do as much as possible to protect yourself. I highly recommend this to you also, whether on the course or on a boat or where ever you are.

I have had small skin cancers removed three times now, because I did not take the right precautions early on. Protect yourself. It is dangerous not to so.

The big hat actually became part of Butch's signature or logo, because he was ahead of his time with it.

John Gehrisch, sporting a big hat

He has also pulled pranks on people for many years. But they also retaliate and get him back.

For example, Butch told me about the time he went out to the practice range to prepare to play a tournament. It was a rather hot day, and as he was warming up, he felt perspiration running down his forehead. He picked up his towel, wiped his forehead, and continued to hit balls.

Soon after, again he felt perspiration, grabbed his towel, and wiped his forehead again. Continuing to hit, and again feeling perspiration on his forehead, this time he just took his forearm and wiped his brow.

He looked at his arm, and it looked strange. It did not look like it should after wiping perspiration off. He took off his big round hat, and looked inside.

All Work and No Play Makes John a Dull Boy

It seems that one of his competitors in the clubhouse had put Vaseline on the inside sweatband. As planned, it was melting! LOL

We used to play quite often with Bill Johnston, a former tour professional who played the Masters three times and the British Open twice. I call Bill my AD (adopted dad) because he reminds me so much of my dear, departed father. Bill and his wife JoAnne, Butch and his wife Pam, and my then wife and I used to take turns selecting a restaurant that none of us had ever tried.

Well, it was our turn to choose the restaurant, and I suggested the Hyatt Regency in downtown Phoenix. It has a rotating restaurant at the top.

I verified no one had been there, and I made reservations for us.

Everyone met at our house, because we had a Cadillac Escalade with the third row back seat. All six of us could fit comfortably in this one vehicle.

We pulled up to the Hyatt. Because it was downtown with limited parking, they provided valet service. We were told we should get on the elevator, and, of course, go to the top floor. The elevator did not go very far before stopping.

It seems that *check in* was on the first floor, and there were quite a few people who wanted to share our elevator. We all pushed to the back. Butch, Pam, Bill and JoAnne were pressed against the back wall. My wife and I were jammed against the rear sidewall, letting the elevator to pretty much fill up. It was a large elevator, and I would guess approximately twelve more people got on with us.

The typical silence ensued as the doors closed, and everyone began watching the numbers check off as we passed floors. Suddenly, Butch broke the silence.

He said, "So, John what did the doctor say?"

I was a little surprised, and it took me a second or two to figure out what he wanted. So, I played into it as best I could, thinking as fast as possible.

"Oh, Butch," I replied. "He said it was dorkulosis!" (Dork-u-losis)

I said it really quickly so it was hard to comprehend. One man smiled. I have a feeling he was a doctor and new immediately this was a joke. The others did nothing, but we knew they were listening.

"Really!" Butch responded. Then he asked, "Is there anything they can do for it?"

I said, "NO! Once you have it, you have it!" I paused and began to cough, simultaneously struggling to spill out, "It's also very con… cough, conta… cough, conta... cough, contagious! Cough."

I paused before I began to cough, finally spilling out the rest of the word, "Contagious!" All the while I was still coughing.

It was hard for all of us to keep a straight face as people literally began to push buttons to get off that elevator prior to their actual floor, so they could select a different lift to their room.

One man looked at me harshly. If looks could have killed, I would have been dead on the spot. He was the last to exit the elevator. After getting out of the elevator he turned and glared at me. I can remember it like it only happened yesterday.

I had the feeling that daggers were being hurled at me from his eyes, while he thought to himself, "I cannot believe you would expose all of us to *dorkulosis!*"

He was still standing, looking at me as the doors closed. Once the doors sealed, we all began to laugh.

Hole # 12

Physician: Heal Thyself

"Knowing yourself is the beginning of all wisdom."
\- Aristotle (384 – 322 BC)
Greek philosopher

Too many people marry for the wrong reasons. Too many people, especially women, get married because they feel their biological clock is ticking.

Or maybe they feel they want children and are getting too old and need to move on it. Or maybe their parents are pushing them because they want to see them married or want to have grandchildren. Or maybe their siblings are all married, and they are the only one left in the family who is not yet married. Many people feel they are not complete because of outside influences.

Ultimately they jump into a "non-organic" marriage that really is not right and ends up in divorce.

Many people seek a relationship like the one that they knew as a child, such as an abusive relationship. One evening, while in a bar, I watched the most beautiful young lady get treated like she was dirt beneath the shoes of her boyfriend. He walked away.

I just had to ask her why she allowed him to treat her like that. I wanted to know what had drawn her to him. She said that she had always been attracted to "bad boys." Why would *any* woman *want* to be treated with such disrespect and public humiliation? She could have had any man in the bar, and there were some who would have treated her really well. Yet, she deliberately and willingly accepted horrible treatment.

I knew the answer before I asked the next question.

"If you don't mind," I said. "I would like to ask a very personal question. Was your father abusive to you when you were a child?"

She hesitated for a minute and then looked at me almost in shock that I would ask her such a question. Still, she then answered in a single word. "Yes," she replied.

"I thought so," I said. "Sweetheart, there are good men out there who would love you and treat you well, if you open yourself up to it. I think you would far more enjoy being treated nicely and respectfully, if you just tried it."

I told her it was nice chatting with her. I walked away before her boyfriend came back, so not to cause her any further problems for even speaking with me.

This is another of those cases where a person needs to be healed before being capable of being ready for anyone else.

What we should be seeking is a spiritual relationship with someone we can feel like we have known our entire life… Someone with whom we almost anticipate their next word or thought or desire.

Reaching a spiritual relationship is harder for men than women, because a woman's brain can go in so many directions.

For example, if a woman guesses that a man is thinking about sex, she has a 50/50 chance of being right! I just had to add a little levity here, even though it is likely accurate.

When you are tuned in spiritually with your mate, you do not mind being with them 24/7. It is almost like living with yourself. So, the point here is that *we* must be healthy first to have a spiritual, "organic" relationship with anyone else.

If we are *not*, we will attract what you are used to. This could mean someone who cheats on you. It could mean someone who is abusive. It could simply be someone who is just not a proper fit for relationship harmony.

Remember, there are four basic things that can be the cornerstones for causing divorces or relationship break ups. These are killers in a relationship. They must be avoided at all costs if you give value to your significant other's feelings and desire a *Happy, Loving, Long-Term Relationship* with them.

1. **Indifference** - That is when your partner treats you like you do not matter. Indifference can include cheating. Basically, they just do not care about you, your desires, or anything about you, for the most part.

2. **Neglect** - That is when your partner takes you for granted. They take better care of their car, job, or dogs, for example. Basically, they seem to value everything more highly than you.

3. **Violence** - This includes both physical and verbal violence. Like physical abuse, the way they talk to you can be abusive. They may talk to you in a way for which they would be arrested if they spoke to the police the same manner. If they talked to their boss this way they would be fired. If they talked to their friends the same, their friends would have nothing to do with them. They just assume that their mate will and should take it, and not leave them.

4. **Contempt** – This is evident when a mate shows little or no respect for the other or tries to make the other feel "beneath" them or not worthy to be in the relationship with them. This can be manifested even with facial expressions and responses, rather than words. We see this in such simple ways as the rolling of the eyes, showing the feeling of "what a stupid thing to say."

Golf Gimme 12:

Playing Augusta and the 2004 Masters

Our good friends, Billy and Shirley Casper, hosted my wife and me at the Masters in 2004. Annually, they rented two homes in the area for the week. They would invite family and some friends to stay with them and share the tickets to the tournament that each Masters Champion gets.

They told us that they would take the master bedroom in one house, and we would get the master bedroom in the second house. The regimen was that everyone would meet at their house for breakfast, go to the tournament for the day, and then return for dinner again at their house.

Once I confirmed with them that we would go, I received a call from Billy. He said, "Now that I know you're coming for sure, I'd like to know if you'd like to play Augusta with Gay Brewer and me?"

I said, "Let me think about it, and I'll get back to you."   I'm joking!!

I immediately said, "YES!!!"   It's every golfers dream to play the Augusta National. It was one of my unattained goals in life. I never got to play in the tournament there, as I never reached that level of success as a professional. But, Billy said we would play on Sunday before the practice rounds started.

I don't know if you've ever gone to the tournament, but if you haven't, it should be extremely high on your priority list if you are golf lover. The golf course is much hillier than you can see on TV, and the greens have much more undulation than is apparent on the TV screen.

The only time I ever saw the golf course on television look close to how it looks in real-life was the year they broadcasted in 3-D. It's a shame they stopped broadcasting in 3-D, because it gives the viewership a more accurate idea of what the course personality truly represents.

Anyway, we flew into Atlanta, rented a car, and drove to meet the Caspers at the houses they had rented. We were shown to our bedroom in the house next door. These are two very nice homes that they rented. The next day, Billy and I went to the golf course.

I got to drive down Magnolia Lane towards the clubhouse with the former Masters Champion.

Few people get to do either of those things. Billy even snuck me into the Champions locker room while we were there. It's different than I expected, as it is an extremely small locker room. But each winner has their name engraved on their locker. The prestige comes from *being* a winner in the first place, and thus, having your own locker where your winner's green jacket is held for you each year.

Billy and I walked outside, and I saw the green and white umbrellas that you see on television. The first thing that went through my head was, "Wow! This really exists." It sort of felt like I had been watching a soap opera for years. You know the feeling of it taking on the sense of reality as you watched, but you knew it really wasn't?

We were then introduced to our caddies and were escorted with our clubs to the practice range. I was warming up, and Tour Star Colin Montgomery walked over to the area next to me.

He introduced himself before beginning his warm-up, as if I didn't recognize him. He talked to me some, then began his own routine. He was extremely friendly. Collin has received a bad rap here in the United States by many people as not being friendly. That could not be further from the truth based on my experience.

After I went through my normal warm-up procedure, I was told we could proceed to the first tee. Billy asked me if I was ready.

I said, "Oh, yes."

As I walked off the range, a number of Masters Champions, like Fuzzy Zoeller, for example, said "hi" to me. I was honored that these guys even remembered me. Though I was a professional, I was not even close to their achievements.

We arrived at the first tee and realized that the tees were covered to protect them so they would be perfect for the tournament. There was an area of maybe 12 or 15 feet at the very end of each tee that was not covered from which we could play. I was going to be playing Augusta from the tip of the tips. I was going to see every inch of this golf course.

L to R: John Gehrisch, Billy Casper, Gay Brewer at Augusta Nationals

As I said, Gay Brewer, another former Masters Champion, was going to be playing with us. He walked up and introduced himself, as if I had never seen him before this moment. I guess modesty is a common theme for great champions.

We all hit our drives down the fairway. Because of my various physical issues, I was past my prime by a long ways, but I still was over 50 yards past these guys off each tee. This was purely because of our age difference.

I had played with Billy many times, and I knew that when it came to his chipping and putting, he had not lost his touch. He would be brilliant, as always, evening things off a lot when we reached the green.

I was able to par the first hole which was a par four. Billy and Gay both bogeyed the hole, because they could not reach it in the two regulation shots required.

The second hole was a par five with a bunker strategically placed on the right half of the fairway right were my ball was going to land, so I favored the left side. My ball slid into the rough, but I was easily able to play it.

My first mistake came on this hole. Billy was out in the middle of the dogleg left fairway watching.

My caddy said, "Hook the ball right-to-left as much as you can."

Before we teed off, I had asked my caddy how long he had been working at Augusta, and he had told me 19 years. I thought to myself that I was really lucky to get such an experienced caddy.

Little did I know that he was nothing but a bag carrier and would cost me four strokes before the round was done.

I guess my caddy underestimated my ability, because when I hit the ball right-to-left around the corner, Billy yelled, "That's in the creek."

I yelled back, "What creek??"

There is a creek that runs through the woods on the left that should have never been in play for me under normal circumstances. I should have walked up and looked at the shot before I hit it. It was my own fault in hindsight.

I thought this caddy knew what he was doing. I was able to salvage a bogey, but I had lost one stroke to par already after two holes, because I listened to my caddy without doing my homework.

As the round continued on, I quickly learned that I could not listen to my caddy's reading of the greens either. I was on my own on the Augusta National.

But my claim to fame that day was that I walked off that golf course with not one single three-putt. I swear I'm going to mount that putter in a frame someday for nostalgia purposes.

We came to one of the holes, and I asked my caddy what the distance was from where my drive laid in the middle of the fairway. He said it was 200 yards and that I needed to hit it right at the TV Tower. As far as I know, I was the first to put a nine wood in the bag on tour. My nine wood would travel exactly 200 yards, so I knew I had this golf shot.

I made a good strike, and my caddie said, "That is off the green."

I said, "What? You told me 200 yards, and I know that's what I hit it?"

This was a mistake I made. He had told me to hit it "right *at*" the TV tower, but for some reason my mind processed "right *of*" the TV tower.

My ball had hit the green, but there was a huge false front runoff in the front part of the green. When I walked to my ball and looked at the pin, the green was almost as high as my shoulders.

I could see the green sloped severely left-to- right also.

I asked my caddy, "How far left do I need to hit this?"

He said, "About three yards."

When I hit the shot, I actually pulled it left an additional three yards.

I immediately said, "Oh, I pulled that left."

Billy Casper's son, Bobbie Casper, who played on a foreign tour at one time and was a great golfer, was caddying for his father. Standing near the flag, he yelled back, "No, this is perfect. Watch this!"

I watched the ball curl back to the flag and stop about 5 feet above the hole, a perfect distance. I was able to make the putt and save par. Had I hit where my caddy had directed me, I would have been down were Billy and Gay ended up.

After my play, Billy Casper chipped from above the green, barely missing the flag. His ball trickled for what seemed forever, eventually stopping about one hundred feet from the pin.

I had not seen Gay hit his approach shot, but he was also down were Billy was. I really was very lucky with my shots for most of the day, especially considering that I did not know the golf course.

As many times is Billy and Gay had played that golf course, just a slight malfunction could put them 100 feet away to putt, as on this hole, for example. That is what Augusta can do to you.

When I completed my round on Augusta, I was four over par. I was thrilled to have played that well never having seen the golf course, and knowing that my caddy had cost me four shots. Plus, I was walking off with *no* three-putts, which is really saying something at Augusta.

I'm going to take that and run! If I never play there again, I cannot ruin what I did. LOL

The Golf Pro Has Heart

On Monday, Billy and I walked the front nine together. And Tuesday we walked the back nine. Billy did not like to get out on the golf course during the tournament, because he becomes a distraction as people would rush to meet him.

The stories Billy shared as we walked were incredible. When we walked through Amen Corner, it just felt right to whisper when we talked. It felt like walking on hallowed ground.

I told my wife that I wished I had had a tape recorder with me that day, so I could've recorded the things Billy told me.

I suggested to Billy that he play the golf course with the Golf channel or somebody who would be recording, so that he could tell his stories. I know that would've been very popular.

He liked my idea, but to my knowledge he never got to do it. He became sick during one of the Masters weeks, and he eventually passed away.

One story he told me was about Ben Hogan playing with Claude Harmon during one of the Masters tournaments. They came to the 12th hole which is a dangerous par three. Many times the Masters has been lost on this hole.

Claude Harmon, a good friend of Hogan, struck his ball and got a hole-in-one. Ben Hogan never said a word. Hogan stood up and hit his shot about one foot from the pin. They walked across what is now called Hogan's Bridge and onto the green. Claude pulled his ball out of the cup, and Hogan made his birdie putt.

As they walked off, Hogan never said a word about Claude's hole-in-one. They walked up to the 13th tee and hit their drives. They walked down the hill and across Nelson's Bridge and were walking down the fairway when Hogan finally spoke.

He said, "You know, Claude, I cannot remember the last time I made a 2 on that hole."

Claude said, "Ben, I made a 1."

Hogan said, "You did? Congratulations!"

I tried to understand what had taken place there. I wondered if he was playing a head game with Claude.

Was he saying, "Hey, you just got a hole-in-one, but you only beat me by one stroke?"

I also had heard his concentration levels were beyond imagination. I wondered if he just didn't even realize that it had happened.

Many years after that day, Hogan was asked about the incident. Mr. Hogan smiled.

"I knew that he had made a hole-in-one," Hogan said. "I always felt it was my obligation, as a golfer, to watch my playing partner's ball. I never watched them swing, but I watched the ball. He knew that I knew. I was just teasing him, but it did make a great story."

How right Mr. Hogan was! This story has been told over and over since 1947, when it happened.

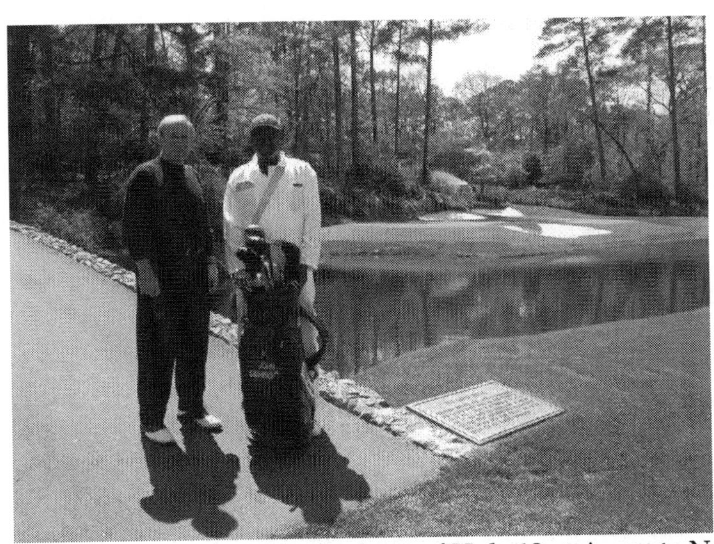

John with Idy on Hogan's Bridge in front of Hole 12 at Augusta Nationals

Billy remembered every shot he made in his final-round the year he won the Masters *and* every shot his opponents made. He replayed many of them for me as we walked the golf course during those two days.

I loved Billy Casper. I miss him terribly. I can't believe that I cannot pick up a phone and call him. I did not do it nearly enough when I could have.

Left to right: Bobby Nichols, John Gehrisch, Billy Casper

He and Shirley and his whole family made us feel like members of their family whenever we were around. I never saw him be anything but gracious and humble around people. He and Shirley are Mormons, and my respect for that religion grew a lot after knowing them.

I know he went through a very tough time during part of his golfing career. He had a food allergy that caused him tremendous pain and discomfort. His wife was a saint and backed him and his mood swings. Many times he could only play one out of three or four tournaments because of it.

How many tournaments could he have won if only they had recognized the problem earlier? Once it was diagnosed properly, he began to eat all-natural foods. He also started eating buffalo meat, which is how he got the nickname Buffalo Bill.

Butch Baird and I have a company called BBJMGolf ventures (www.bbjmgolf.com) with another man that makes golf memorabilia. This is really more of a hobby, but we did an all-wins piece for Billy. It can be seen on our website.

I was looking at his piece with him one time, and I was admiring all of his wins. I asked him of which win he was most proud.
I fully expected he would choose the famous U.S. Open win over Arnold Palmer where he came back from so far behind to win. But he didn't say that.

Arnold Palmer and John Gehrisch after walking a hot Augusta National

He said it was the win when he was the Captain of the Ryder Cup. That shows how much the Ryder Cup means to these guys, especially back in that era. I think it means a lot now, but not as much as then, which is a shame.

The Golf Pro Has Heart

Jack Nicklaus' suggested change of including all of Europe for the European team, has helped level the playing field and made it much more competitive and interesting, as the U.S. used to dominate almost every year. This was a good change and typical of the sportsman that Jack Nicklaus is.

By the way, the 2004 Masters was the year Phil Mickelson won his first major. In fact, I was sitting with my wife on the 18th hole when he made his winning putt.

As he was looking his putt over, I yelled out to him, "This is your year, Phil."

I don't know why I did it. Somehow, I just knew. Normally, I would never have said anything. My wife was surprised when I did it because it was out of character for me.

I just would never take a chance on breaking anyone's focus. But sure enough, Phil drilled the putt into the cup. My comment probably did not matter one bit, but I like to think that I put positive thoughts of confidence in his mind that may have played a small part in his making history.

(I am seated second from left in the front row.)   Photo Credit: Golf Digest, 2004

Golf Digest called me a short time later and asked me if I had received my copy of the magazine yet. I had not.

The representative told me that I was in the background of the photo when Phil did that gigantic, vertical leap of his, after making his putt to cinch the Masters for the first of what would become several times.

The magazine rep blew the photograph up for me. I had Phil sign it for me, and it hangs on my office wall today as a reminder of one of the greatest weeks in my life… all thanks to Billy Casper.

Hole #13

Typical Differences Between Men and Women

*"Any fool knows men and women think differently at times, but the biggest difference is this.
Men forget, but never forgive; women forgive, but never forget."*

-- James Oliver Rigney, Jr., a.k.a. Robert Jordan (1948 – 2007)
American fantasy author

How many times have we heard men and woman make fun of the opposite sex and their idiosyncrasies? If I only had a dollar! LOL

In fact, we *are* different. Very different. But is that really a bad thing?

I recognize that we all get frustrated at times with the opposite sex. At work, at play, at home. It happens. It is a fact of life.

But is it really the opposite sex that we are frustrated with or are we frustrated, at the moment, with a specific person? Are we being overly judgmental at times? Are we stereotyping? Don't we also get frustrated with people of the *same* sex?

Or is the real problem that we do not recognize, understand, or value our differences?

One of the main reasons that marriages fail, or, for that matter, succeed, is how a couple understands, respects, and handles the differences they possess as members of the opposite sex. Most marriages can break down largely because of this fact.

Typical Differences Between Men and Women

Let me explain further what I mean. Let's begin with the fact that every women's body and every man's body are different because of the chromosome patterns.

The mental, physical, and emotional differences are so extreme between the sexes that without a concentrated effort to comprehend and respect them, a *Happy, Loving, Long-Term Relationship* is virtually impossible! Some of these differences are probably known to you, but some may not be. Some we have mentioned already but let me details just a few that are known to me.

Approximately 80% of women tend to more right-brained, as referenced earlier. That is the side of the brain where feelings, emotions, nurturing, and the relationship part of life is orientated, motivated, and operates.

Approximately 80% of men tend to be more left-brained, as also referenced earlier. That is where the competitiveness, fact finding, information sorting, language and more logical processing and rational side exist.

Additionally, roughly expressed, women's brains are 8% smaller than men's, but they have more interconnections. Women perform better with the "bigger picture" and "circumstances" type of thinking, while men tend do better on specific spatial thinking, including pattern prediction, involving objects and their spatial relationships, as well as problem solving.

Generally speaking, the back of the brain handles perception, and the front of the brain handles action. The left hemisphere of the brain is the seat of logical thinking, while the right side of the brain handles intuitive thinking.

The findings lend support to the view that males may excel at motor skills, while women may be better at integrating analysis and intuitive thinking.

Having said all this, women can be bilateral in their thinking. This means that they can access *both* sides of their brain simultaneously, whereas men tend to think literally, favoring only one side at a time.

Other, simpler things include that in the USA, men tend to deteriorate physically about 10% every year after the age of forty, whereas women tend to deteriorate 2% every 10 years. That is part of the reason women typically outlive men.

Men tend to have 40% muscle in their body, as related to their body weight. Women tend to average only 20% muscle. I have not seen recent numbers, which may have changed since the years when I first read them. This is potentially due to such things as the rise in both gym memberships and fitness awareness worldwide.

Important differences caused by nature also exist. For example, little girls talk more than little boys. Typically that continues into adulthood. Women also tend to relate to other people on more of a personal level, whereas men tend to be more competitive by nature.

Further, a woman usually defines herself though the relationships that she develops, whereas a man identifies himself though accomplishments in his work or sports. Women usually are much more in touch with emotions, while men concentrate on facts. Usually, when a woman tells her mate about her bad day, she just wants to vent and be heard, whereas a man wants to just fix it and move on.

Men often complain about women talking too much. Apparently, there's a biological explanation for the reason why women are chattier than men. Previous research has shown that women talk almost three times more than men. It turns out that, on average, a woman speaks approximately 20,000 words a day, versus about 7,000 words a day spoken by the average man.

Of course, a man only *hears* about 2,500 of those words. LOL. Okay, I might have embellished the last part of that statement, but most ladies would likely agree that I am probably not that far off.

Actually, studies show that men probably hear only about 15% of the words spoken by their female partners.

Additionally, women generally speak more quickly and devote more brain power to speaking. Till now, researchers haven't been able to biologically explain exactly why.

Regardless, women now have an explanation for their gift of gab. They can silence critics with scientific research indicating a biological reason why females talk much more than males.

Women's brains have higher levels of a "language protein," called FOXP2. This has been established by a research study at the University of Maryland's School of Medicine.

This helps us appreciate major differences, generally speaking. Perhaps it also helps bring understanding to some of my points.

Of course, men and woman also have physical differences to deal with every month.

So, how can members of the opposite sex ever hope to have a successful marriage, or meaningful relationship, or even be friends, considering our dramatic differences?

Well, ladies. Truthfully, it is not all on you, but it is easier for this part for you than men.

Why? Because of what I already mentioned. Remember what is referred to as a "chemical bath?" The fact is that a woman spends most of her time using the right side of the brain, where the skills of having that intimate relationship exist.

The right side of your brain is the epi-center of primary rational, feelings, language, and communication skills. This is where our intuition, imagination, detailed work, appreciation for fine art, feelings of love, and so many details are remembered.

So, naturally women were created with the capacity of two critically important abilities. First, they have the intuitive desire to build a relationship that is meaningful in life.

Second, women have the capacity to identify a potential intimate and healthy relationship better than men do. Basically, women have a built-in relationship or marriage manual in their brains. They only need to learn to access it.

However, men do *not* get off Scott free!

Men, as I have said before, are cursed by God to be visual by nature. But we are also vocational.

Therefore, we can benefit both ways if we take the time to learn meaningful communication skills. We discussed this earlier, but men do not dwell in the area of thoughts about relationships. Men are typically more interested in fix-it magazines or golf or the football team rankings or the like.

Most men do not have (or do not know how to tap into) the right-brained skills of women. Still, there is no excuse *not* to develop better communication skills.

This is especially vital if you care about your partner in life.

Men, who do not have the romantic mindset, can become *non*-typical. To do this, a man needs to tap into the marriage manual in his mate's brain. It is right there in your own home.

Golf Gimme 13:

Hawk Attack!

Many times, Butch Baird and I have pulled pranks on people. A favorite is one that we call, "The Hawk." This is also the prank that our "victims" most frequently request we pull on other friends of theirs. They love the thought of somebody else having this happen to them.

I have seen many different reactions when the hawk does its thing. Some people dive onto the green. Some people, like Shelley Hamlin, scream. One guy threw his putter down and ran off the green, pausing only to inspect his shorts to see if he had wet himself. *That* may have been the second funniest one.

The funniest reaction has to be the story I will share next.

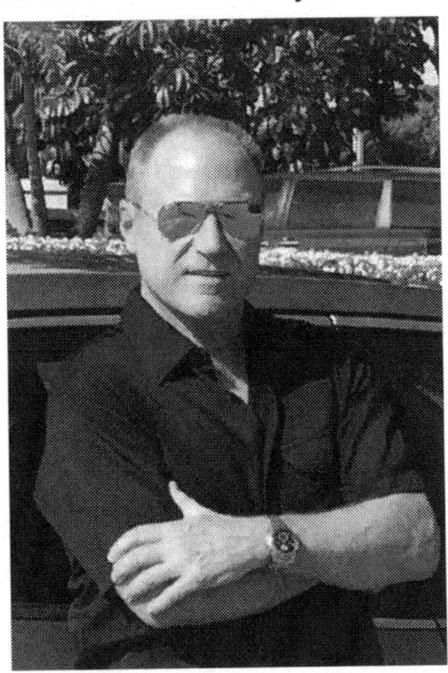

John, proud of pranks

First, let me explain how the hawk works. Typically, Butch will ask me if I warned the people we are playing with about the hawk on the next hole. I will respond that I had not. He will recommend that I tell them about it for their safety.

Dutifully, I will tell them that the next hole seems to have a hawk, which must have a nearby nest that it is protecting. I make sure they are aware that the hawk has been swooping down on golfers on the green while they're putting. Occasionally, it has come so close it has knocked off people's hats.

We will proceed to the next hole and, ultimately, the green. When we approach the green we act as if we're looking in the trees for the nest and the hawk. Occasionally, we have actually seen a hawk, which makes the story even more plausible.

Then, just prior to one of the players leaning over their putt, we will pick up the flag stick, holding it from the end opposite the flag. We sneak up behind the person, and swish the flag quickly across just above their head, which makes a flapping sound that is very similar to that of the wings of a hawk flying overhead. For example, if we go right to left, we start about 6 feet right of the person and end about 6 feet left of them. They don't notice because we do this while their head is down, looking at their ball. Suddenly, they hear the sound of the hawk swooping in over their head and then quickly leaving. It can sound very realistic.

The reactions are varied and priceless. One guy said, "I could feel the talons going into my scalp."

So, the day I mention here was a day at Desert Mountain. Jim Marsh, a friend who used to live in Scottsdale was visiting and met up with me to play a round of golf. Butch, Jim, another guy, and I were playing in our foursome.

On Hole number seven Butch said, "John, have you warned Jim about the Hawk on the eighth hole?"

"No, I haven't, Butcher," I said.

"You probably should do it," Butch responded. Butcher is a nickname I have picked up from his wife, Pam.

So, as Jim and I got into the cart we were sharing and began our drive towards the tee for the eighth hole, I remembered that I had not "gotten" The Butcher in a prank for a while. You see, we not only prank others, we also like to "get" each other… a lot.

So, I explain to Jim exactly what was going to happen, so he knew ahead of time.

"Jim," I said. "I will get Butch to be the one to pass the flag over your head to make the flapping noise. Right after he does it, I want you to drop your putter, stand straight up, grab your chest like you're having heart attack, and fall to the ground."

Jim questioned me, "You want me to actually fall onto the green?"

"Exactly, Jim," I responded. Jim reluctantly agreed.

We all had made our shots to the eighth green, which was a par three. When it was Jim's putt, I signaled for Butch to grab the flag, as I was, intentionally, standing a ways away from it.

Butch picked it up and snuck up behind Jim. Just as Jim was pulling the putter back, Butch swooped the flag making the Hawk wings' sound, as we have done so many times.

Jim dropped his putter on command, stood straight up and grabbed his chest, said, "OH! OH!" He fell to the ground as instructed.

Butch rushed in and looked down at Jim. I can still see his hands spread widely holding the flag stick in both hands with a horrid look on his face wailing, "NO! NO!!!!"

I began to laugh, Jim began to laugh, and Butch became aware that we had pranked him!

I said, "You really thought you had caused a heart attack, didn't you?"

Butch responded, "Dammit John, you got me good on that one!"

I replied, "I realized that I had not 'gotten' you for a while, my friend. For some reason, I just felt the need!"

We both laughed, as this is *so* much in both our natures and always in good fun! Lord knows that Butch has "gotten" me enough times!! LOL

Hole #14

Respecting Differences

*"We may be wired differently as men and women,
but some needs are parallel **human** needs."*

-- Cathy Burnham Martin (1954 -)
American author in *The Bimbo Has Brains*

Why is it that couples have such a hard time communicating with each other? I don't mean simple conversations. I mean deep, open-up-your-heart conversations? After all, your mate is supposed to be the most important person in the universe for you!

Yet, there are so many things that go unspoken. So many needs are being unfulfilled. There is so much hidden frustration. Why do we have trouble at times sharing our true feelings with each other?

Why is it easier to just let it lay, and hope that someday it will magically somehow repair itself, when deep inside we know it won't?

Have you ever asked yourself, "Why can't he (or she) feel what I am saying?"

Has a person of the opposite sex ever acted like you were speaking in a foreign language when you tried to tell them something that was important to you? Why is it such a struggle to communicate some things, especially when it is an important concern to you?

Maybe it is time that we realize and acknowledge that women do speak a different language than men, and vice-versa. I have heard men say that it is impossible to talk with women. I will never understand them.

And when I go into the other corner of the room, the women are saying the same thing about men! Maybe as John Gray PhD once said, "Men are from Mars, and women are from Venus!" This has been an ongoing discussion all through history.

With all the technological changes, why hasn't anyone come up with a translator app for our cell phones for this problem?

(Hmmmmm - make note to self to do this. LOL)

Let's look at the typical difference of a man and woman when shopping, just as an example. One time, before my divorce, I took my wife out for what I call a mystery date.

I used to do these periodically for her to keep our romance alive. I love romantic things and places. I would tell her when the date would be, what time, how long we will be gone (hours, days, or weeks), what kind of clothes to wear (or bring), and when we would be home. Everything else was a surprise and arranged for her to enjoy. It was one of my ways to say, "I love you and appreciate you."

So, on this particular day, I arranged for us to have a simple mystery date brunch on the water. These do not have to be anything fancy, by the way, if you would like to use the idea.

There was live entertainment, and it was a stunning day. I guess I even managed to arrange for a porpoise to swim by in the waters we over looked while we ate. Okay, truthfully I am not sure how that happened, because I had never had seen it before or since, but I was happy to take credit for it. After a wonderful brunch we walked around a few nearby shops.

When we first met, I had a substantial, high-end glass paperweight collection that she loved just as soon as she saw it. She said that she could get into collecting them herself. I had commented that if I was a girl, I would collect glass perfume bottles. She was not sure what type I meant.

A week or so later, I was able to show her what I was talking about, and she loved the idea and began her own collection. These items I speak of are made by artists by the way. They are collectibles.

Anyway, on the day of this particular mystery date, we stumbled across a couple bottles made by her favorite artist in one of the stores. I told her that I wanted to buy her one. So, I suggested that she select the one she liked the most, which she did.
A few stores later we walked into a dress shop. Now, my wife was a former model with a stunning figure.

The owner spotted her, and I am sure it was a sales gimmick also, but she said, "OMG! I just got some new sun dresses in, and I have been dying to see them on a figure like yours. Would you mind trying a few on?"

Of course, she said, "No." Wrong! Very few women do not like trying on new dresses, right?

I sat down and began to watch the show. As she modeled dress after dress, I decided to tell her to pick out two, as she could use them. She always looked awesome in anything.

While she was in the dressing room trying on the 8th or 10th dress, I asked the owner what kind of discount she would give me if we took them all. She said 25%. I said that I was sure she could do more like 40%, as I knew the mark up in clothing.

She acted like she had to check her cost, left, and came back, agreeing to the deal.

My wife emerged and asked, "Which two do you like best?"

I surprised her when I said, "We are going to take them all, babe."

She said, "What?!!?"

I replied, "You can use them. Take some to your mother's and leave them there, so you'll have them when you are there."

(This was during a time when she was there a lot because her mother was ill.)

Now here is a difference between typical men and typical women. As we walked to the car, I felt that we had had a wonderful day and that I had made her feel special.

Now, I fully expected to go home, maybe watch some golf, and perhaps get a special thank you from her for the Mystery Date. LOL

Instead, the dresses were put into the car, my hand was grabbed, and I was dragged into the shoe store next door with a request to get shoes to match each of the dresses.

Let's just say that the day was ruined for me because all that I had done was still not enough for her. Maybe because we were on a different planets. I was on Mars, and she was on Venus.

My point is that men see things very differently. A woman can try on fifty dresses and ask if you like each one.

Even if you say yes to them all, she may drag you into 5 more stores and may or may not even buy anything in the end. Many times it is the process for her.

I happen to like shopping, but most men do not. Most men just want to conquer the project by making a decision and moving on or getting home to watch sports on TV.

Most, not all, women love the shopping experience. Most men are different. The sooner we all accept this, respect it, appreciate it, and accommodate it, the sooner we can all be happy.

Gary Smalley has a bachelor's degree in psychology and said in one of his seminars that 80% of women are right-brained, and 80% of men are left-brained. For the purpose of this book, we will accept that this is correct.

He states there are many important differences caused by nature existing between men and women. Many you know. Maybe a few you don't. Regardless, understand these are critical for relationships to work.

Here is just one example Gary gave. A woman comes home from a tough day at work. She wants to vent and tell her husband what happened to her that day. All that the 80% of right-brained women really want, is for her husband to listen and be sympathetic and understanding of what she went through.

But instead, 80% of men are left-brained, and, therefore, are fixers or conquerors. Typically, they will begin to tell her that all she has to do to solve the problem was to do such and such, so she will get out of his ear and let him get back to watching the game or news or whatever he was doing.

She is not satisfied with this at all. She does not want him to fix it. She wants him to be her friend and listen. Listen like her girlfriends do. He does not understand this at all.

The natural instinct of 80% of men is to conquer the damn thing and move on. You hear me say this a lot... Men and their conquering nature.

But can you see the 180-degree difference between most men and women just on this point alone?

Can you see where a breakdown is imminent, and over time this can cause a breakdown of their entire relationship, causing them to drift further and further apart?

She feels rejected by him, and he feels like no matter what he says, it is going to be wrong, when all he had to do was shut up and listen. But no one has ever told him that.

Ladies, hand him this book and have him read this chapter!

Men, I ran across a blog posting that I am copying here that might help you understand this point, to aid your relationship in the future. Listen to this man's experience.

kinklu says:

March 10, 2014 at 1:40 am

"My wife and I have been married over 46 years. We almost got divorced a couple times but backed out of it well before taking action. We have no secret except for one. She likes to tell me about things that bore me like her shopping trip or what kind of hamburger she bought our grandson for lunch.

"I used to pretend to listen while was on the computer or reading. One day she came home all excited about what the grandkids had done and I had to wait for the computer to download or something.

"So I turned in my chair, looked directly into her eyes and listened while asking intelligent questions about details. I'll never forget the way she lit up. It was magic! She treated me like I was a prince.

"The part that really did it was to look intently into her eyes like I was only interested in her words and nothing else. I'm not always able to do this every time, but I have discovered that if I do it frequently, it changes our relationship!"

- - - - - - - -

See what I mean! This really works! Why? Because men and women are different. The sooner both sexes learn that, and respect it, appreciate it, the sooner we will both have better relationships.

# Golf Gimme 14:

Casting Call

The week after the Turtle Bay Championship Tournament, my fiancée and I were scheduled to take the week off and spend it in Maui. Many of our family joined us, because this is when we'd scheduled to get married.

A very strange thing happened, and, honestly, I don't even remember what caused it. I just remember going to bed that night and experiencing excruciating pain in my right wrist. It was like someone was stabbing me periodically with a knife. Just as I would start to go to sleep, I would leap out of bed from the unanticipated pain.

My fiancée wanted to go to the hospital, but, being a typical man, I said, "It will probably be alright in the morning. I will tough it out."

The next day did not show improvement, but, later that night I was jolted out of the bed with pain again. Now I suggested that I should seek medical assistance, or we would never get any sleep.

We found an all-night clinic. After X-rays and various tests, the doctor said, "To be honest, I don't know what this is." He went on to say, "It could be carpal tunnel, it could be a pulled tendon, or it could be a pinched nerve. I am going to give you an extremely strong anti-inflammatory injection in the buttocks. I will also prescribe a pain medication and a sleeping aid. I want you to buy a wrist de-mobilizer at the pharmacy and wear it non-stop until this stops."

He gave me a piece of paper prescribing the de-mobilizer. Once I put it on, all I could do was picture myself in our wedding photos in my tuxedo, saying, "I do" it this stupid thing. I was not happy about that.

A couple of days later, the condition still had not improved. My bride said that she and her brother and sister-in-law we're going to go play golf and wondered if I wanted to ride along.

I said, "You know what I'm going to do? I'm going out with my clubs, and I'm going to try to hit some golf balls. Let's see what happens."

My bride said, "It's just my opinion, but I think you are out of your my mind. You'll probably end up in the golf hospital."

I said, "One of two things will probably happen. Either something will let go in my wrist, or I *will* end up in the hospital. I'm going to go find out which."

A few hours later we were on the range hitting balls. I had a horrible time keeping my right-hand in the shot, which promoted a slice or left-to-right ball flight.

I decided to try to hook the ball, making the ball move right-to-left, to counteract the slice. I hoped that it might go straight enough that I could play.

It came time to head to the tee, and my bride asked me what I was going to do?

I said, "I'm going to try to play."

Her brother and sister-in-law were listening. The general consensus was that I was crazy.

"Gee, you've always known that," I said and laughed as we moved off towards the first tee.

I actually did draw the ball a little bit right-to-left on my first drive, but I made par on the first hole. I don't know what caused it, or on what hole it happened, but I no longer felt the pain.

Soon afterward, I was hitting the ball normally again.

I ended up shooting four under par for 68. No one thought it possible in our group, including me. But I was back!!!!!

Oh, yes, and *no* wrist de-mobilizer in the wedding photos! LOL

Hole #15

JAG Formula for a Happy, Loving, Long-Term Relationship

I heard a woman say once, "I am looking for a one-in-a-million man.
I need to begin to eliminate the other 999,999!"
It is rare that someone finds the perfect life partner quickly.
Like a flower, usually you have to plant many seeds
to have the perfect flower appear.

-- John A. Gehrisch
American Entrepreneur and Tour Golf Professional

I was certainly not going to make you wait until the book's end to reveal my formula for a *Happy, Loving, Long-Term Relationship*. Though I have doled out gems of wisdom along the way to this point, I do not want to appear as if I'm only giving it to you in bits, like Hansel and Gretel dropping breadcrumbs for you to follow.

Further, I should note that JAG has long been a nickname of sorts for me, since the letters are my name's initials. Thus, let's now delve into the heart of the matter.

JAG Formula:

A Happy, Loving, Long-Term Relationship = [2 Givers + God + Values + (Trust + Security) + Support + Friendship + Spouse's Family + Affection + Lover (Intimacy) + Romance + Laughter + Understanding + Forgiveness + Attraction + Communication + Commitment] – [Betrayal + Lies]

Before breaking down the components further, I think you can see why it is hard to find a person who brings all these things to the relationship.

Usually they are missing at least one or more of these, which always weakens the relationship chances of being truly happy and loving for the long term. Let me touch on each of the JAG Formula keys.

2 *Givers*

Let me start with the fact that this is one of the most important Keys. IT IS EXTREMELY IMPORTANT!! In my opinion there are 3 types of people in this world: Givers, Takers, and Takers who *think* they are Givers.

1) If two Takers marry, they will never ever be happy long term and almost always end in divorce!! They may stay married, if they both have been raised by their family to not accept divorce no matter what. But they will be miserable, and likely end up in separate bedrooms, at the very least. You may know couples like that.

2) If a Giver and a Taker marry, they may stay together also if raised to do so by their family, but they will likely end in divorce, as well. However, this marriage will likely last longer because a Giver also tends to be a more committed type of person. A Giver wants to fix what's broken, before giving up easily. A Giver always hopes things will get better. But they rarely do. Things usually get worse! Here is why.

I will use an analogy to illustrate this. Let's say you own a house and are at home one day when there is a knock at the door. You answer, and there is a man standing there.

He says, "Good morning." He then proceeds to explain to you that he is a home maintenance expert. As he passed your home, he happened to notice that you have paint bubbling around your windows.

He explains how it will begin to crack and peel and begin to retain water. Then your window frame wood will rot, and you will have an expensive repair problem on your hands.

As he explains that you will have to replace the frames or possibly the entire window eventually, he also notes that he just happens to have time today. For $200 he can run down to the store to get some paint and supplies, and then he'll scrape and prime and paint where it needs it. He adds that this, ultimately, should save you a lot of money in the long run. So, you tell him, "Okay."

Later, you hear him working outside. Eventually, there's another knock at the door. You answer, and the man says that you already have water in the wood. If he paints over the top of it, and you allow it to stay, it will just rot. Your window could fall out. He says that for another $800 he can get additional supplies and remake your window frame.

You don't want your window to fall out, right? So, you reluctantly approve.

After some time passes, you hear another knock. When you open the door, you now hear the man explaining that he has now discovered peeling paint under your eves of the roof. For $300 more, he can scrape and paint them while he is at it, so that does not become a serious problem for you later.

Do you feel your wall of defenses beginning to build? Do you feel yourself withdrawing from trusting this man and your relationship with him, perhaps feeing taken advantage of by him?

This is what happens with a giver and a taker in a relationship.

The Giver gives, and the Taker takes. The Giver gives, and the Taker takes. The Taker gives very little back, and if they do, it's usually only when they want something in return.

The Giver does not give for the sake of receiving something back, but over time the Giver begins to feel taken advantage of, and the Giver begins to build a wall of resentment. Over time, that wall gets higher and higher. The Giver usually begins to withdraw more and more. They typically start to stop giving altogether.

Then the Giver begins to become someone they are not meant to be, which makes them unhappy. The Taker also becomes unhappy, because they are no longer getting. As time goes by, they both become increasingly unhappy. The couple starts to drift apart until, eventually, one files for divorce.

Sometimes it is the Giver who files, because they reach a point where enough is enough. Even though the Taker is still getting some things, they can be the first to file, because they want that larger amount of giving back again.

The Giver personality tends to be a more committed person, who tends to stay too long in this situation.

3) A major secret in the formula to true happiness is 2 Givers!! The first Giver gives to the second Giver. That makes the second Giver want to give back, which is already natural for them. When the second Giver gives back, that makes the first Giver also want to give back again, even more.

This becomes a constant, never-ending circle for life. Look at any married couple that is really happy after 50, 60, or 70 years of marriage. They constantly talk about the <u>other</u> person and everything their mate does for them… <u>and</u> how much they adore them!!

I saw this in my own parents. I just wish I had been astute enough to figure this out years ago!

Once, my father told me that each person in a relationship must "give in" 65% of the time. Interesting and great advice. If all people would do that, the world would be a peaceful place.

In my opinion there are far more Giver women than Giver men.

I think two factors contribute significantly. First, even women who do not have children possess a natural motherly instinct. I also think the number might be 80% women are Giver personalities, and 20% of men are Giver personalities.

My parents kiss and toast to 40 years of marriage

Why? I believe it ties directly to the left-brain/right-brain distribution that I talked about in earlier chapters. I do think it is an important point to understand and consider when dealing with the opposite sex. I don't think women even have 20% of single men to choose from to find a true Giver Personality Man, because they get snapped up so quickly by astute women or women who have read this book.

You may recall that I mentioned earlier how women have "the knack" to recognize good men when they see them. Unfortunately, women also have to settle for Takers, if they are too focused on age or geography or wealth or certain other factors.

If a woman is more flexible, she can find a true Giver Personality Man with patience and careful due diligence.

However, women need to be careful, because Takers are masters of doing what it takes to get what they want. After all, they have been doing it their whole life.

So, beware, because Taker Personality men *and* Taker Personality women can fool you!!

They give, in order to get what they want, *appearing* many times to be a giver in the relationship! They identify the things you like.

Some do this consciously, and some don't even know they are doing it. They do what you like until they get what *they* want, which might be *you*.

Then it stops, and they become the real person they are inside. This happens because they perceive that they "have" you or what they want. So, they no longer need to work to please you.

Have you ever heard a woman say something like, "I just don't understand what happened to the wonderful man I married. He used to bring me flowers for no reason at all. He opened doors for me; he pulled my chair out for me. Now he does none of those things."

Well, that can be because the Hunter and Taker were coming out in him "back when." Men were born Hunters. He baits his trap and lures in the prey. In this case, it is the woman!

Once the trap has sprung, and the prey (the woman) is trapped, he moves on to other goals… usually career, other women, or something else.

That can happen at different stages for different men. It might be sex for some men. It might be engagement for others. It might be marriage. But a Giver continues giving for a lifetime because it is in their nature to be that way. He/she actually gets fulfillment and happiness seeing their mate be happy. As long as it does not stay a one-way street, of course, as I said!

I have seen it happen to a man by the woman also. The Taker Personality women knew what the man liked and did it all to get him to marry her. Once they were married, it all stopped!

In those 50-year relationships, where couples are still madly in love, you will see 2 Givers Personalities *every* time!!

God's Guidance

I won't say you have to believe in God to have a *Happy, Loving, Long-Term Relationship*, but it helps. At the bare minimum, adhering to the guidance He has given us is huge.

I believe that God made woman for man. In the scriptures, God took one of Adam's ribs and made woman.

I believe that a good woman is God's greatest gift to a man, and a good man is God's greatest gift to a woman.

This should be honored as such. "How?" You might ask. God's instructions are clear. Yet, many times they are misinterpreted or interpreted the way someone *wants* them to read.

Every couple I have seen, that abides by his commandment on how a marriage should work, has been very happy.

Many times we receive this gift from God, but we are blinded by greed or other things, and we miss the opportunity for true happiness in a relationship.

I am not someone who pushes faith down people's throats, but God gave us specific instructions that make relationships work. God told us that a woman is to love, honor, and obey her husband, holding him above all things and above all others, including children, parents, family, and friends. The man is to be the head of the household, but he is to love, honor, and hold his wife above all things, including children, parents, family, and friends, also.

What does that mean? And what does it mean for the women to obey? It means a man should always listen to his wife's desires, wants, and needs and to place her in a special place in his life and heart. He should always try to make her happy. Only if her desires are such that they could hurt the family unit financially or its safety, should the man step in and override her desires. Ultimately, he is responsible to love, provide, and protect the family unit.

Some men do not understand the true meaning of the woman obeying him, and try to become a dictator. I do not feel that is God's will. Seriously, how should a man who should value his wife more than life, in good conscience be a dictator to his life partner?

You might find it interesting that I once inquired of a Catholic priest, "How would I know when it was right for me to marry a woman?"

I believe his answer was a good one, however, not totally complete. He said that I would know when I was willing to die for her.

As illustrated by this book, I think there is much more to it than that. But I also know that in my previous relationships I would have died for my woman without hesitation.

Do what I have explained here, and even if you don't believe in God, I am confident you will have an excellent chance of happiness, especially if you have the other items in the formula. Again, I have seen this in every single happy long term relationship I have studied.

Values
This means that the couple needs to give the same importance to things. A few examples include:
- Do they both want children, or not?
- Do both like to travel, or is one a homebody?
- Do both believe in God, or is one an atheist?
- Do both like dogs or cats?
- Do you agree on how money will be handled?

Even simple things can cause problems. For example, my ex had a cat before we married. She offered to give her cat up to a friend, so it was not anything I had to even ask of her. But it could have been a problem because I am allergic to cats. Maybe I could have gotten injections if the cat had been important to her, but such things are potential issues. They need discussion.

We can't overlook the issue of money. How you handle money is an extremely important topic for discussion as money is one of the primary causes of divorce.

Trust and Security

These are similar, yet different and so important! What do I mean? I think of trust more in terms of infidelity. Also, remember what I have said before.

Being monogamous is not natural. It is not automatic. It is a choice. Are you both willing to make that choice for life?

Security is more about the confidence and commitment of both people to love and value the partnership for a lifetime under all situations, good and bad.

Are they together through all difficulties the couple might face and any storm that confronts them?

Security strengthens a relationship, especially when they know they are fully committed to truth.

Conversely, insecurity can destroy a relationship extremely fast. If you asked your mate how secure they feel in your relationship, how do you think they would answer on a scale of 1 to 10?

If their answer is less than 10, ask what you can do to move it to 10? This is important. What would be your answer to them if posed with the same questions?

Believe me, under most circumstances you have the power to create the relationship you want and the life you want, if you are <u>both</u> willing to put in the effort. Be certain you are committed to this process.

When you are selecting a mate, be certain that the partner you have chosen is just as committed as you are to your common goals. One person will rarely, if ever, be able to achieve or maintain this alone. Nor is one person likely to be able to rekindle it should you have it and lose it.

Support

Support flows from our inner being. This is how we show respect for a mate's personal passion, belief, or activity.

Even if it is something in which we don't have a personal interest, if we fail to "endorse" our mate's interest, then we have failed to support it.

We discussed this issue of support earlier, and it is an important key to a relationship's good health. If we are not sincerely in support of our mate's passions, beliefs, interests, or activities, then we are likely working to undermine them.

Working against our mate's personal interests may not even be a conscious act on our part. However, if we are not with them, we may well be "against" them in quiet, unspoken ways. This would be very detrimental. Get on board!

Friendship

I think most people hope to marry their best friend one day. This is the ideal situation. However, do not be confused. This does not mean you should marry your best friend just because they are your best friend, especially if, though they are of the opposite sex, you are already in a heterosexual relationship.

It means if the other things in the formula are present, you have a strong attraction, and they are your best friend too, then this is a major score.

Why? Primarily, this is because you likely enjoy similar things, enjoy spending time with each other, and probably can communicate well together.

This is really important because if you are <u>not</u> best friends, one or more of the other ingredients in the formula may break down over time, causing the relationship to break down.

For example, maybe something happens sexually where you can no longer be intimate. Even though there are major medical breakthroughs to help, it is still possible.

So, having that special someone in your life that you actually enjoy doing other things with will become even more important.

Spouse's Family

For the best details on why this is an important key, please refer back to Hole #3 - Parents Set an Example.

Affection + Lover (Intimacy) + Romance

These keys have many similarities. While sexual needs of men and women are an extremely important part of the "lover" to whom I refer in the formula, the differences are remarkable between men and women when it comes to affection and being lovers.

In many ways a man is like a gas stovetop. He's quickly ignited and warmed up ready for action.

A woman is much different. She is more like a crock pot that needs time to warm up and cook. It can take a woman hours and even days being treated as a valuable person to her man, before she becomes "emotionally available" to him.

Translate that as meaning she gets a mutual desire for sexual intimacy.

Men "enjoy" sexual variation. Women, by nature, "need" sexual variation.

Men can be happy doing the same thing over and over again. Many women will tolerate redundancy because she loves her man. But one thing that will catapult a woman to cheat, or at least think about it, is the desire for creativity and something different than the last time, and the time before, etc.

It is good for a man to hold his girl and talk, even before kissing her to begin love making. It is OK for a man to ask her what she is in the mood for to please her better. A woman's mood or desires can change daily. Sometimes this is because their body is different that day. May she just finished her monthly cycle and is sore for example. At times she might be in the mood for tenderness. Other times she might be in the mood for something more aggressive. Ask her to tell you.

If the situation does not lend itself to tis before things heat up, then he should ask as they begin. So as to not spoil the mood, her answer can be short, and the man's response should be short. Something like, "Got it, Babe" or "Thank you, Sweetheart."

A real man will not be intimidated by being told what to do, but rather will embrace her inputs. Remember, communication is critical to a happy relationship.

Most men have no idea about this. Approximately 80% of women crave the need for touch and in a nonsexual way. For about 80% of women, intimacy does not begin in the bedroom at all, but in act of affection, trust, truthfulness, kindness, thoughtfulness, romance, touching, talking, all that nurtures the desire in a woman for her man.

UCLA did a study on the health of women. It found that women need to be touched 8 to 10 times per day in a nonsexual way from her loved one to remain healthy, emotionally as well as physically. Additionally, the study revealed that some highly driven "Type A" men could add up to two years to their life spans by just slowing down at the end of their day and giving their wife a long gentle hug when they walked in the door after work.

Touching someone also lowers a person's blood pressure and can literally energize or improve one's mood if they are hurting or down emotionally.

Spending a romantic dinner or candlelit picnic or just holding hands when you walk is not only romantic, but can help build that bond in the bedroom.

Let me just touch a bit more on romance. Remember what I said about date night previously? You could try my Mystery Date Idea to keep things romantic. This does not have to cost a lot of money. Try something simple. Maybe a picnic and glass of wine on a hill where you can watch the sun set alone on a blanket would be nice. Make it something for which you have to put in an effort. This shows it's special for the two of you.

Check out my blog where you can share your ideas for loving mystery dates and other experiences on my website:

www.GolfProHasHeart.com

Let's get creative. If you are a woman, please also do this for your man. What we are trying to do is encourage romance and togetherness.

Laughter

I hope that people know how important humor is in a relationship. People do not have to be comedians, but we do need to be able to laugh at each other and ourselves to enjoy life.

Seek someone with whom you can laugh!

I had the nicest thing said to me one time by a woman I went out with on a few dates. Let me quote her, because she honored me so with her words. To this day, this remains one of the nicest things anyone has ever said to me: "I have so much fun being with you. If they are right, that laughter increases how long a person will live, then if I can be with you, I truly think I will live forever!"

Understanding

Try to be understanding and seek someone who will try to
be understanding with you. Everyone has a different
point of view from time to time. Everyone also makes
mistakes. The question is whether a mistake is a character
flaw, or intentional, or accidental?

If we align ourselves with someone with similar values, and
you will find you both have fewer times that you will have
the need to be understood better. Sometimes we just did
not understand what our partner was attempting to say or
do. Make sure you don't jump to the wrong conclusions.
Get the facts. Use the right side of your brain for this.

Forgiveness

Beyond understanding, we have an inherent need to both forgive
and be forgiven.

Okay, so we are all human. When we have said or done something
hurtful to our mate, we must sincerely apologize to open the door
for them to give us their sincere forgiveness.

Plus, if they have slipped, we need to truly forgive them, and not
just in "word." This needs to come from our heart.

Check out the companion book to this one, called *The Bimbo Has
Brains*. Cathy Burnham Martin has an exceptional chapter
explaining *how* we can give and *why* we *need* to give "Genuine
Forgiveness" to others, as well as to ourselves.

Attraction

How does your partner look to you? How do they smell? How
do they taste? How do they dress? How do they eat? What is
their personality like? Is their sense of humor comparable with
yours? How does their family fit you and yours? Can you travel
long distances in a car without fighting?

Make you own list of important things that will ultimately make
you attracted to, or repulse you from your mate.

Communication

We've covered this in detail in another section because it certainly requires far more space than a couple lines or paragraphs here. Remember, good communication is a *critical* part of the formula.

Commitment

Throughout my formula you find commitment is the glue that holds it all together. Without commitment, relationships crumble.

Minus, or take away, betrayal + lies

By now, you know that I believe this is an absolute "must" for any solid relationship. It goes hand in hand with trust. Betrayal or lies will kill affection so fast your head will spin. If you betray or ever lie to your mate they typically *will* find out sooner or later.

So, here is my formula again for that *Happy, Loving, Long-Term Relationship*, the one we all desire.

JAG Formula:

**A Happy, Loving, Long-Term Relationship =
[2 Givers + God + Values + (Trust + Security) +
Support + Friendship + Spouse's Family +
Affection + Lover (Intimacy) + Romance + Laughter
+ Understanding + Forgiveness + Attraction +
Communication + Commitment] – [Betrayal + Lies]**

Golf Gimme 15:

Turtle Bay

The Professional Golf Association only allowed 144 players to attempt to earn one of four spots as qualifiers, so you better bring your best game. Typically, I had to shoot a 68 when attempting to get in as a qualifier. In the first year that they moved the Champions Tour event from Maui to Oahu, the winds were so strong that the qualifiers were able to get in with a score of 70. It was one of the highest scores I ever saw shot to qualify.

That year, I sat having breakfast in the restaurant at the Turtle Bay Hilton where the tournament was being played. We were talking to Hubert Green and his wife at the next table.

A large plate glass window was behind them overlooking part of the ocean and a mountain in the distance. Over Hubert's head, I noticed a few wind electricity generators sitting on the mountaintop. Not one was working, and I found it strange that they were not taking advantage of the winds.

I asked the waitress why those generators were not running, and she said that the wind was so strong there and changes direction so violently, that they could not keep them operational. Yet, those were the conditions in which we were about to play.

On the day of my practice round, the air was very calm, so I didn't know just what to expect for the tournament. The good news is that I always was a good wind player. In fact, I typically finished higher among the competitors when winds were blowing, so I wasn't very intimidated. I actually saw it as an opportunity.

The Golf Pro Has Heart

On the first tournament day, the wind started to blow pretty hard. Around the 15th hole, I experienced one of those dramatic wind direction changes. I had a medium iron into a front center pin. As I hit my shot to the green I was four under par. The wind was directly in my face which was preferred. I struck the ball, hitting a low trajectory to try to keep it under the wind as much as possible, and it began heading directly toward the pin.

Suddenly, the wind gust blew a strong 90° from my left. I watched as the ball was guided off of the green into a pile of rocks on the right of the green.

I watched to see where the ball bounded, fully expecting the ball to ricochet off of the rocks. I saw nothing. I asked my fellow playing partner if he saw where that ball went after hitting the rocks, but he had not.

After scouring the area for my ball, we determined that it went into the pile of rocks and never came out. I went back to my original spot as required by the rules and struck a second shot that ended 3 feet from the pin.

I thought to myself, "Worst case, I lose one shot here to par."

When I walked up and surveyed my putt, I noticed the 3-foot putt was going to break at least 18 inches, and, if I hit it the slightest bit too hard, I could easily have eight or 10 feet left because the greens were stinting green speeds between 12 and 14, which is typical for PGA tournaments.

If you don't play golf much, that's like putting on linoleum. I hit my putt very carefully, narrowly missing and leaving myself three feet below the hole.

I made the next putt and walked off the green losing not one shot, but rather two shots to par. One strike of the ball can dramatically change your score in this game. That's why we concentrate and work so hard when we are over the golf ball out there.

Billy Casper and John at Hole 11 at Augusta National

Hole # 16

Discussion Questions to Improve Your Relationship

"I am a great believer
in not pushing each other's "buttons"
just because we know where they are!
That's part of trusting each other.
We need to trust that our vulnerabilities and challenges
are safe with the person we love."

-- Cathy Burnham Martin (1954 -)
American author in *The Bimbo Has Brains*

I was asked recently if I could describe what I thought I would feel with my ideal women, and after some thought I wrote the following:

"She is my love, my Everything. With every day that passes by, it seems like I discover something new to love about her. She makes me laugh, think, and try to be better person for her and myself. She makes an incredible difference in my life. She touches my heart in a way I never before thought possible.

"My love for her is deep, true, developing more each and every day, proving she was made for me. She stole my heart from the moment I met her. When she appeared in my life it felt simply natural to throw open the doors to the most private parts of me and openly share them with her.

Discussion Questions to Improve Your Relationship

"Her love moved into the very essences of my soul, and never leaves, because I trust her completely. Our love arises, nearing sensory overload, without the slightest advance warning. Our senses are heightened; ordinary becomes extraordinary; simple becomes spectacular; common becomes astonishing, and the whole experience feels calming, comfortable, and a perfect fit.

"With all my heart, I feel that our love is mystical… unique, special, magical, and heaven sent. If anyone asked me what the happiest day of my life was, I would close my eyes and feel a joyful tear trickle down my cheek as I think back to the day when she first told me she loved me with all her heart.

"She is my confidant, my world exploring travel companion, my lover, and my best friend. We can discuss anything and everything without arguing, well into the night. Living without her is merely an existence, being shallow and empty and hardly worth doing.

"I love her not only for who she is, but for who I am because of her."

This is not fantasy. This is the result of much thoughtful development. If you not yet in a relationship, spend careful time, thought, and care in choosing your partner. If you are in a relationship, and it does not fulfill you both, think about the many possible ways you can make steps forward to improve it.

Ask yourself and each other the following questions to help get you started.

- Would spending more time together improve our relationship?
- If so, how much time is needed, and how could we spend it?
- What is the most convenient time of day for us both to commit to it?
- Do we agree that more and better conversation could improve our relationship?

- What is different between my idea and my mate's idea of meaningful communication?
- What might I have done in the past to ruin past meaningful conversations?
- Is there anything in the past that I have done for you in previous conversations that you felt made me a 10 mate?
- How am I doing in the area of meaningful touch?
- What can I do to make myself a 10 in your eyes, if I am not?
- How would you rate me in communication skills on a scale of 0-10?
- Do you feel we have arguments, or discussions?
- If you feel we argue sometimes, what can I do to make it more of a loving discussion?
- What needs do you have to grow more as an individual that am I not nurturing… that I could be more?
- In your mind, what would be a 10 date night for us?
- What could I do to ruin that date night?
- What are some ways you feel I could communicate more effectively?
- What could I do, to better understand what you are experiencing when you are hurting?
- What could I personally do, to make our conversations together a 10?
- Is there anything that I do, that makes you fearful of me?
- What do you cherish most about our relationship?
- If you could change 3 things about me, what would they be?

Golf Gimme 16:

How to Put Spin on the Ball Like a Pro

I am not looking to make this a golf instructional book. But most people who have played golf for years will answer the next question wrong every time. "Where should my divot be in relationship to the ball's position before hitting it?"

Putting backspin on a ball is not necessarily simple. You need the proper technique and the right conditions to do it. You also need to play the correct ball for your abilities.

Making a ball spin back when dropping on the green is like putting backspin on a cue ball in billiards. It also will provide more power to your golf shot.

To properly do it in billiards, you hit downward on the bottom half of the cue ball with significant force. Striking the ball at a downward angle, and increasing the velocity of the cue stick as it moves toward impact also helps, just as it does on your golf ball.

In golf, it means that you strike the golf ball on a descending blow before hitting the ground. Therefore the club continues for a few moments into the ground after the ball, so the proper divot is after the spot where the ball laid, not before it where so many people think.

I tell people that golf is a game of opposites. When you want the golf ball to go up, you strike down. When you want the ball to go left you swing to the right putting a right-to-left spin on the ball, curving it like a baseball with a right-to-left spin.

If you want the ball to go to the right, you swing right-to-left, placing a right-to-left spin on it.

So many times I see people trying to hit up on a golf ball to make it go over water or trouble of some kind. That normally places a topspin on the ball making it dive downward right into the trouble they're trying to avoid.

To put backspin on a golf ball, the goal is to "pinch" the ball between the club and the ground. You typically also want to hit downward on the ball with a fair amount of force, so that you accelerate through the ball.

You should learn to make clean contact on the lower portion of the ball. It helps to have a clean club face with some grip left on its face, although I have seen a good ball strikers put a lot of spin on the ball with a completely smooth club face, proving technique is critical.

Remember, some golf balls are designed not to spin, reducing the error, helping a higher handicapper score better by keeping their ball out of trouble at times. Using a low spin golf ball will also result with less spin on the greens.

The combination of all these factors — angle of attack, force, and clean contact — places backspin on the golf ball.

Coordinating all these factors in your swing is why it takes proper technique, learned only through good instruction, good basics, and a lot of practice.

Conditions will also affect ball spin. Listed below are the three conditions you need before hitting a spin golf shot.

If these factors are missing, it is better to allow for the ball to run out and not expect consistent spin.

- Conditions must be fairly dry, except in bunkers where wet conditions make the ball spin more

- You must be on low cut grass such as the fairway or a hard surface such as some dirt or clean, hard sand/fine stone

- Greens have to be in good condition, somewhat soft and receptive

I use backspin when I need to hit a chip or pitch-and-stop shot. This type of shot is best used from inside 30 yards or when you have a problem or obstacle, like a sand bunker, rocks, or water between yourself and the green.

This is where you do not have the option to hit the ball on the ground and need to hit a higher shot over the problem obstacle. If you put enough backspin on the ball, it should take a bounce or two and stop. Normally, I choose a high-lofted wedge for this.

For example, I know I can chip a ball with my 60-degree wedge 2/3 of the way to the flag where it will bounce 2 times and stop dead. I adjust that for more roll out if the greens are hard or if I use a less-lofted club, seeking more roll. You just need to practice, and determine your own results.

The higher the loft, the harder it is to be consistent. Use lower loft, like maybe a 9 iron, to allow for more run when trying to score your best if you are a higher handicap. Start with this until you can hone your abilities.

Professionals use a high-spin/soft-cover ball for better control around the green and for pitch-and-stop shots. I recommend using the same for anyone who really wants to learn the shot.

A good tip is when you address the ball, have more weight on your lead foot. The ball is played back towards the inside of your back foot. And make sure your hands are set a few inches ahead of the club's face to deloft the club. Try to maintain that position at impact to ensure a firm crisp descending contact of the ball, which imparts more backspin.

Hole #17

Another Letter and My Reply

"It kills you to see them grow up.
But I guess it would kill you quicker if they didn't."

-- Barbara Kingsolver (1955 -)
American novelist and poet

Dear John,

Hello! You know, I'm a bit upset, and I don't know what to do. I had a really long and hard work day. Today I had a lot of patients and I was tired.

Before I went home, I had a call from my mom. Unfortunately, I was not able to talk to her all day, because I really had a lot of work. I told her that when I got home - I'll call her!

But maybe it's just not my day?! When I got home, I saw that my neighbors were at our building. You ask me why? Because it is the eternal problem - Our neighbors love to flood each other, and sometimes it's possible to hear their arguments, and I can't sleep.

Now they tried to find out who is at blame for their problem, and I ended up involved in part of their problem.

When I came into my apartment, my mom called me. You know what happened next?!

The conversation was:

Mom said, "Do you think it's normal to promise to call and not keep your words?"

I said, "I'm sorry. My neighbors had a problem, and they needed my help!"

Mom then said, "I don't care what problems your neighbors had. I'm worried about you. You know that Kiev metro is a very unsafe place! You were supposed to call!!!"

I apologized saying, "I'm sorry. So, how are you?"

My mother responded by saying, "I didn't expect this from you!!! I thought you were a serious woman, Nastya!"

Then she just hung up on me. I tried to call her back again and again, but she stopped responding to my calls. I am in shock!

John? What am I supposed to think and to do? You know that when she called me, she was on the street. I lost my peace of mind! What should I do? Maybe something happened? I am thinking tomorrow I should give up my work and go to her? My parents are the most precious thing that I have in this life! But now I have lost my sleep! I feel guilty, and I'm afraid that something happened to her!

Can you help me?

With hope in my heart…
Nastya

And here is my reply.

Nastya,

I can understand why she would worry if it is a routine that you call every day at the pretty much the same time. I hope you will find there is nothing wrong, and think that will be the case.

I also feel her reaction was childish to hang up on you and not answer when you called back. Personally, I think it is time you have a heart to heart talk with her and make her realize you are 27 years old and no longer a child.

You are a grown woman with your own life, and I feel you need to stop the daily contact, especially at a set time. That may be hard for both of you, especially at first, but you should stay strong for the good of your relationship.

Remember, time spent should be based on quality, not quantity.

I also know that your goal is to marry a man from the USA, which means moving to another country. How could you possibly do that with this attachment you two have to each other?

I think she would not support such a move, and probably she would put you into the situation of having to choose between her and the man who you fall in love with and could offer you happiness. That would put you into an unfair position, and if you ultimately chose not to move to him, you have been very unfair with him.

I believe you need to begin to condition your mother to let go and allow you to have a life of your own and have her also begin to accept that you are looking for a man abroad, and that means you will ultimately be moving further away from her. It does not mean you cannot come back to visit, or her to you.

None of those things mean you love her any less, or care less for her, or that she should stop loving you. It simply means that all children are supposed to be raised to survive on their own, think and make decisions on their own, and any parent who does not prepare their child for that does them an injustice.

Along with that comes releasing them to the world like all animals do their young in the wild. If she loves you, which I am sure she does, she needs to support you in your quest for happiness and independence. Anything less is unfair to you.

She just needs to realize what she is unintentionally doing. It is hard for a mother to let go.

But also, no parent is around forever, and a child cannot live their life happily or successfully through their parents.

The next thing she might try to put pressure on you to have children as a replacement for you as you pull away some. I see people all the time have kids because their parents want them to.

Many times they later wish they had their freedom back to enjoy their own life because they did not really think about how their life will change and revolve around their children for many years.

You have told me you want to be free to travel and explore parts of the world. More and more couples are finding that they live so much better without having to spending so much money and every waking moment scheduling around their children's activities. Especially if they seriously think about what is involved with raising and paying for a child, usually giving up many life experiences like travel for instance.

Let me be clear please. I am not saying you should not have children. I just am saying to think it through carefully before doing it. It consumes much of your life for at least 18 years. A girl said to me once, "I have heard plenty of girls say they want children, but I have never heard one girl say they wanted to raise a child!"

How true! Because most people do not think that far ahead.

Food for thought,

John

Golf Gimme 17:

The Azores Tournament

During the time period when I was playing golf professionally, I was asked to play in a tournament off the coast of Portugal on one of the Azores islands a few years in a row. It was sponsored by SATA Airlines.

First came two days of practice rounds, followed by a Pro-Am tournament, where we professionals were assigned four amateurs with whom to play. On the following two days, the amateurs played a two-day net tournament among themselves.

As professionals, we played three days after the Pro-Am. Then we would leave the next day, so I never had a chance to see much of the island. In the last year I played I had to withdraw because of a back injury.

So, we had a chance to drive around and see the island more. It's a beautiful place, one you might enjoy going sometime.

The first year, during my practice round on one of the courses we would play during the tournament, I was approaching the second hole. It was a par 3 with 150 on the card and tee sign. I hit an 8 iron about 150 yards.

So, as I approached the tee, I was thinking 8 iron. I then processed that it was uphill.

With my caddy at the Azores

So, then I started thinking a 160-yard shot, which is a stock 7 iron for me. Then I realized it was a back pin, adding 10 yards. That would make it about 170 yards, which is a stock 6 iron.

Wait! It is into the wind. Better add a club making it a stock 5 iron for 180 yards.

OMG! I am in Azores. They use meters here. Now I must add about 10%, or play it 188 yards, rounding to 200 yards. I just went from an 8 iron to a 9 wood, and that could be short because the 9 wood hits it higher, so I better play draw or a slight right to left shot which adds 5 yards for me. Another option would be to add one more club to be safer, because the pin was on the right. If the ball did not work right to left, I would miss the green and short side myself, which is normally a no-no to any good golfer.

WOW! I was zeroing in at 200 yards. What an adjustment had to be made! About 5½ clubs needed to be added. Welcome to International Tournament play and the Azores.

My wife had a great experience playing in the amateur tournament, following the Pro-Am day. She was playing with three men as a team that was drawn by a committee. She was not a long-term golfer as she had taken it up shortly after meeting me, but she had been improving a lot. She knew the rules better than most because of playing with me and other professionals.

Right after we'd first met, she rode along in my cart one day while I was playing and decided she wanted to try it. This was the first Pro-Am in which she had played. She absolutely hated playing in front of people. So, this would be interesting to see how she handled it!

I finished my professional round earlier than she finished her amateur around, so I was waiting for her to come in on the final hole.

The bar overlooked the 18th green, which was a par three hole on the course she was playing. I was watching for her from that balcony outside the bar on the second floor along with about 75 other people.

I thought to myself, "What is she going to do when she sees all the people watching everyone finishing on 18?!?"

Finally, her group appeared at the tee.

The three men played first from the men's tees, and none of them hit the green with their tee shot. Now my wife walked to the women's tees with all eyes upon her.

I wondered if she would even be able to hit the ball, because I knew how nervous she got as a newbie with people watching. To my amazement, she struck the ball onto the green, being the only person in her group to do so.

A huge roar rocked out from the balcony, rewarding her shot. I knew that if she had not noticed everyone before, she certainly was going to now.

The three men hit their balls onto the green with their second shot after walking to it from the tee. She was, by far, the farthest person away, but her ball was laying there in one instead of two shots.

From the balcony, I could see that she probably had at least a hundred-foot putt over a mound in the green with a huge break left to right. I thought if I could see that from the balcony, I wondered how imposing it must be looking from her vantage on the green.

She walked up to her putt with all these people watching. She had her back to the balcony, which was probably a good thing. Still, I knew in the back of her mind she was very aware of the gallery watching. I could not imagine her actually getting that putt up-and-down in two strokes with all these people watching.

She rolled the ball and it went one hundred and three feet, almost going in. The gallery on the balcony groaned loudly as the ball narrowly missed. I knew again she would become aware of the gallery.

She had been a good putter right from the beginning, but I could not imagine her doing what she did under these conditions. She still had three feet with a slight break to negotiate to make the only par for the entire group, and a net Eagle for the team. I thought, surely she would miss this, especially with this much pressure and so little experience.

The gallery grew quiet. In fact, the quiet was almost deafening.

She rolled the putt, and it hit dead center, dropping to the bottom of the cup.

The balcony gallery went crazy. These are the experiences that makes golf special and also bring you back week after week to play the wonderful game. I realized right then and there, when it came to tournaments, she had an ability to play outside her normal zone on many holes.

From there on, anytime I could get her on my team, I did it, because I knew she could birdie or par almost any hole on the golf course.

The first year I played this tournament, I noticed how nervous the amateurs were on the first hole. I remember feeling some nervousness back when I was an amateur and able to play in some Pro-Ams with professionals.

I set out to try to put these three men at ease, because I knew they would not enjoy themselves or play well otherwise. By the end of the second hole we were all joking, relaxed, and having a good time.

Their team did not win the Pro-Am, but they all thanked me for a wonderful day and asked for my autograph and told me how much they enjoyed playing with me. That meant a lot to me. That's really what golf should be about.

The competition is always enjoyable and challenging, but if you can't have a good time and walk off feeling you had a great day, why do it? Why would you want to stress yourself instead?

I have noticed professionals treat amateurs in the Pro-Am many different ways. All professionals need to remember that these amateurs have paid a lot of money to play with us. They also need to remember that without these amateurs supporting the game, there would be no tour and no money to be made. I think many professionals forget that.

I heard a story once about JC Sneed that I don't know for sure is true. Supposedly, he was playing with a team of men in a Pro-Am at Pebble Beach. It may have been the Pebble Beach Invitational that I played for a number of years.

Anyway, the story goes that he played 18 holes with the guys and basically never said a word to them. On the 18th hole one of the amateurs had about an 8-foot putt for birdie. JC Sneed had noticed the Leader Board near the green, and he did some computing in his mind.

The amateur was kneeling down behind his ball trying to visualize the break that his ball would encounter as it rolled towards the hole. He knew it would likely break some to his left, which was towards the ocean. Everyone knows the ball will typically go towards the water because that's the way a green is normally shaped to drain.

The story goes that JC walked over and kneeled down behind him. He said something to the amateur like, "If you make this putt, it's worth about $1800 to me."

He then stood up and walked back over to the side.

Having read his putt, the amateur took his stance over his ball so he could attempt to knock it in the cup. He stood for a few seconds over the ball, not pulling the club back to hit it.

The story I was told continued that he stood straight up and looked over at JC and said, "Let me get this straight JC. If I make this putt, it's worth about $1800 to *you*. Is that correct?"

JC allegedly concurred.

The amateur then turned and faced as though the hole was towards the ocean, instead of 90° from it. He hit the ball as hard as he could straight into the ocean waters. Then he gleefully walked off the green!

Now, I don't know for sure that this is a true story. But honestly, in my opinion, if JC, or whoever it was, treated them that way that day, he deserved what happened. It was a statement from the amateur to him as to what he thought of him and how little he enjoyed the day after paying so much to play with him.

I feel that in all our relationships, whether they are long-term, or short-term, just as in a day of golf, people should be treated with respect and friendliness unless and until they do something where they don't deserve it.

As I have said, a professional needs to keep in mind that he is no better than the amateur with whom he plays. He simply has the opportunity to play golf professionally because people like those amateurs support the game. They should be respected and honored as such.

Arnold Palmer, one of the most winning golfers in history, never forgot why he was out there, by always giving back to the game. I never heard of him being anything but gracious to people. That is why "Arnie's Army" was present, following, and rooting for him in every tournament. He certainly was always gracious and friendly to me.

Likewise, we should respect and honor all people, but especially the important people in our lives, like our mates.

Hole # 18

It Does Exist

I share this next letter exchange, because I believe it's worth reading. I start with the letter that I received.

Dear John,

I am fairly recently widowed. My husband was a pediatrician, still working full- time in the Fort Myers area, when he died of complications from bacterial pneumonia. For 17 years, Jack and I shared a love that many people never find in their entire lifetime! Ups and downs, for sure...ins and outs, absolutely...but the love we shared is beyond my ability to adequately describe in words. It was a world of our own, without perfection but with passion and depth that even amazed us at times, the kind of love that now gives me strength and confidence and faith in the good in people.

Jeannine

Next is my response to her letter.

Jeannine,

First, I am sorry for your loss. There has to be a real hole in your life and heart. Usually, every day gets a little easier, but you will never forget, and you will always have a place for him in your heart, and that is the way it should be.

I wrote something to someone some time back. I am going to look for it and copy it and send it to you. You might find it interesting.

Second, thank you for your earlier comment regarding my book. Yes, I know that type of love exists. My parents were happily married and in love for over 50 years.

I have seen other examples, too. After the failure of my second marriage for reasons I let remain confidential here out of respect for my ex, I embarked on what became a *Life Changing Journey of Discovery*. I was trying to find out why I chose so poorly.

I was only 19 when I married the first time, so there was some understanding there. But I was old enough the second time to know better. I just did not have the information I needed.

There are no classes in school on how to pick a life mate, unfortunately. The things I discovered were real eye openers. I showed some people, and 100% said that I needed to write a book. So, I did. It has not been published yet, and I would like to use what you wrote somewhere in the book. Your letter was beautiful. It was heartfelt. It was meaningful. It was encouraging. I loved it.

I know you are in a very challenging time of your life. Trying to heal is difficult, but you need to worry about you right now.

My advice is not to try to replace your husband. He was unique and his own person. What you had with him you will never have exactly the same with another person. There is no one like him. Let someone enter your life that you enjoy being himself.

My father remarried after my mother passed away from smoking. He told me once that he could not believe he found two women in his life like that. She fit him, but she was different than my mother. I was grateful that she kept my father around longer, because I really thought my father would just give up and die after my mother passed.

My mother was his was his everything. But he found another companion to spend time together with and soften some loneliness. They both did, as she was a widow, just as you are.

Keep that wonderful smile on your face, Jeannine. Your husband would want that.

John

Golf Gimme 18:

Meeting the Prince and Princess of Morocco

One year, I was invited to play in a tournament sponsored by the King of Morocco. The tournament had begun 31 years earlier, when Billy Casper became friend with an earlier King, who had since passed away. The three children that Billy had first known as children, had elevated status now. One had become King. One was the Prince. The daughter had become the Princess.

Billy invited Butch Baird, my wife, some other friends, and me as pros and amateurs to play in the different stages of the tournament. Plus his son, Bobby Casper and his wife, Kelly, we're in attendance. My wife and I flew to New York City to enjoy the beautiful Christmas lights in the snow, before joining Billy and the group at one of the New York airports to travel together.

Left to right: Billy Casper, Ben Crenshaw, John Gehrisch

Upon arriving in Morocco, we were escorted to our own private customs area for clearance because of Billy's association with the royal family. During the next few days, we experienced many things.

We saw how typical Moroccans live in the countryside, after by being invited into a couple's home. We toured their house and observed that they had basically no furniture nor beds. They bathed in a little adobe-like structure in which they could not even stand up. They had no running water.

They were very pleased to welcome us, and very proud to share the breads and butter they had made for our visit. We were led to a table sitting outside.

In my mind, I can still see the many flies that had congregated on top of the butter, but we certainly did not want to hurt their feelings, so we all partook in their offering. The wife served us, all the while having a baby hanging from the front of her body in a sling-like pouch. The grandmother, who also lived with them, sat in the corner hand weaving a blanket.

Later, we were escorted to beautifully lavish, brightly-colored tents sitting alongside a lake. We had a wonderful, catered meal. After eating, the men went to have a practice round on the nearby golf course, while the women enjoyed a camel ride on the beach.

The following morning, we went to the train station for an approximately four-hour ride from Marrakesh to Rabat. We were then taken to our own private room to wait for the embarking. When we boarded the train, we realized that we had our own private railroad car, which we could certainly not begin to fill. Continuously, through the cabin were rows of seating for four people on the right and four on the left, in sections of two facing forward and two facing back. Each couple in our group had their own section of four seats if they elected to sit alone. We were served lunch after the train started its trip, and then we all settled in to relax for the remaining trip.

Butch and his wife, Pam, Billy and his wife, Shirley, and my wife and I chose to sit together in the two sections in the front of the train car, so we could talk for a while. As I sat, I was looking back through the cabin and noticed that Bobby was sitting with his wife about midway back. Kelly was reading in an aisle seat, while Bobby had gone to sleep with his head against the window. I noticed they had a blanket across them. I asked Butch if he had brought his remote controlled fart box with him, and he responded positively. I asked him to give it to me.

I nonchalantly walked towards the back the train passing Bobby and Kelly, verifying that their seating situation was as I thought I had observed. There was a separation between their two seats, just like ours in the front of the train car. I quietly slipped in behind them. I discreetly slipped the fart box under the blanket on Bobby's seat. I then returned to the front and sat so that I was facing backwards.

Butch moved closer to them, making sure that his remote control signal would reach the needed box. He then sat facing forwards, so he could see my nonverbal instructions. Billy was sitting beside me, also facing backwards, so I clued him in on our planned antics. He watched intently.

I gave Butch a nod, and he pushed the button. The fart box produced a small noise. The first sound is small, but as additional sounds are added, it proceeds to become longer bursts of fake gas releasing noises. There is no odor, only noise.

As this went on, Kelly looked up at Bobby in dismay, thinking that Bobby was doing this while sleeping. She looked back at her magazine and smiled a bit as she processed momentarily, then slipped back into concentrating on the article she was reading.

I waited if little bit and then gave Butch another sign. He promptly activated the box again, making it sing out longer this time.

Kelly looked at Bobby with disbelief, turn back forward and hid her face with the magazine she was reading.

Her head began to nod some, as it was apparent she was laughing to herself, but she did not want to call attention to the situation.

Waiting another minute or so, I gave Butch another nod. He repeated the prank.

This time Kelly looked at Bobby and felt the need to shake him and wake him advising him of what he was doing, so that other people did not become offended.

The look on Bobby's face made it quite apparent that he was not happy that she woke him. It was also clear Bobby did not feel he had done what Kelly was claiming. A small, unaligned discussion took place, before Bobby placed his head back against the window and closed his eyes again.

I made sure Bobby had enough time to go back to sleep before prodding Butch to work his magic again.

Again Kelly woke Bobby from his sleep. I could not hear her words because of the noise from the train rolling us down the tracks towards our destination. But I could somewhat tell what they were saying to each other. The conversation went something like this.

"Bobby! You are passing gas!"

Bobby said, "I am not, Kelly!"

"Yes you are, Bobby!"

"I am not!!"

"Yes you are, Bobby. I can hear it! It's coming from right there!!" She pointed towards his ass.

By this time, I am slumped in my chair, doubled over with laughter. I can hardly get my breath. I'm laughing so hard my stomach is beginning to hurt!

Billy, sitting beside me, is laughing so hard he has tears running down his face. Seriously! He had tears running down his face.

I looked at the troubled couple again in time to see Bobby, who had noticed us by now.

He looked at his wife while pointing his finger at us. He then said something like, "I don't know what they're doing, but they are doing something!!!!"

Ah, yes. We let the good times roll.

A few hours later we arrived in Rabat, where the tournament would be held. While there, we experienced many wonderful things. We even saw a snake charmer at the market, just as we'd seen on television. He was playing his music and making this snake weave back-and-forth slightly out of the basket. Because we were there with Billy, we had a government driver everywhere we went. He would escort us to the markets and help negotiate prices if we wanted.

One evening, we were invited to a wealthy carpet shop owner's home for dinner. He was a friend of the Caspers. This gave us a chance see how the more successful people lived. We also got to see the colorful, hand-laid tiles that adorned walls of their home. These folks were extremely friendly and gracious to us. We were shown traditions, including how to properly roll rice into a ball in order to eat it with our hands.

In the hotel one night, I had been invited down for a drink with a few of the other pros. Mark Roe, one of the European pros who had traveled in, had joined the group. We soon discovered that in terms of pranksters, Mark made Butch Baird and me look like rank amateurs.

At one point, Bobby said, "Mark, tell John what you did to John Bland at that one tournament."

Mark began his story. "Okay. Well, John, we were playing on an island where there were no cars. On one of the first mornings, I was standing out on my second-story balcony with a cup of coffee, when I heard something coming from my left. I looked down. It was John Bland on a trike, peddling across in front of the hotel. He then turned left between two cement freestanding posts and continued down the hill to the practice range. He was not moving real fast, and I imagined it might have been his first time on a tricycle.

"The next day I was having my coffee out on the balcony again. I heard a noise and spotted John peddling a little faster past the hotel, turning left between the two posts, and proceeding to the range. That evening I went down and moved the two posts closer together.

"Standing on the balcony the following morning, eagerly awaiting John's arrival, he did not disappoint. This time, John was getting comfortable, if not a little cocky, riding his trike towards the range.

He went flying by the hotel, passing underneath my balcony. Coming to his turn, he proceeded rather quickly. He entered between the two posts with three wheels, but exited with only one, as the back two wheels were removed by the cement posts. As John flew through the air it's rumored that he yelled, 'DAMN YOU, ROE!!!!!'"

I think Mark might have embellished the last part of that story, but I could sure see the removal of those wheels, exactly as he told it.

As I stood on the elevator to return to my room, I held the doors from closing as one of the other guys at the table rushed to share the elevator. Having heard other stories about Mark Roe while I was there, I remarked, "That Mark is a major prankster! He's my kind of guy."

As I waited for his response, I noticed something white on his black sweater in the shoulder area. I said, "What is that white stuff all over you?"

He looked down and realized that Mark had said, "See ya later, buddy," as he'd patted his shoulder with his hand filled with salt or sugar! LOL

The next evening, my wife told me about meeting the princess. My wife was playing in the women's tournament and had hit a rather bad golf shot, not traveling all that far off the tee she was playing. She then topped her second shot, making it only roll 40 or 50 yards. She walked up to the ball and repeated the same thing.

This was not typical for her at all. She was then instructed by her caddy that she needed to move aside and allow the group behind to "play through."

Being a little irritated because she is not normally known to be a slow player, she did as requested.

Watching the group play through, she realized that, of all the people she might hold up on the golf course, she had chosen the Princess of Morocco! It was later explained that the tradition there is that the Princess tees off last of the day, but she "plays through" everyone, finishing at whatever pace she wants.

As I walked up to the last hole of the tournament, I noticed TV cameras were rushing towards our group. I was used to TV cameras so I didn't think much about it. I struck my ball down the fairway and it slid into the right-hand rough slightly. Being filmed as I walk towards the ball, and again, as I hit my second shot, I put the cameras out of my mind and struck the ball 6 feet from the cup. The cameras recorded me making the putt and walking off with a birdie to finish my round.

Little did I know I would later have a first place trophy in my hands that looked similar to a rail from a railroad, but made of pewter with imprints of golf clubs and a flag. That would be fun to get home through a metal detector at the airport, needing a ready explanation.

They were very proud of that trophy. It now is the heaviest in my trophy case.

Prior to the presentation, we attended a First Class Black Tie Dinner party provided for all the pros, their spouses, and amateurs participating in the tournament. As were being served dessert, I noticed some of the pros whispering something to each other at other tables.

Eventually, someone came to our table and told us that all the pros and their spouses were being invited to a private party afterward at the Prince's Palace.

"Oh, my gosh!" I said to my wife, "We're going to the palace!"

As we drove up to the palace and exited the car, we were escorted through the heavily armed guards into the palace. We were free to roam and go into many rooms, but, of course, we were not allowed in the private residence areas.

Every room had either entertainment or food in it.

We were standing in one of those rooms talking to someone when my wife grabbed my arm and quickly pulled me into a different room. I inquired what was wrong and was informed that the Prince had entered the room through a different door. I asked what the issue would be with that.

She reminded me that when a woman is introduced to the Prince, protocol requires her to curtsy. She had never done that before and was not looking forward to doing it for the first time there.

We thoroughly enjoyed ourselves for the evening. As we were getting ready to leave and bidding our friends farewell, another pro called out my name from about 30 feet away.

"John! Have you met the Prince yet?" he asked. I noticed that the Prince of Morocco was standing directly in front of him.

I said, "No, I haven't."

He prodded me to come and be introduced, which I did.

I found the Prince to be a charming young man who is very friendly. Enjoying talking with him, I discovered he had actually gone to university in the United States. Realizing how warm and friendly he was, I could not refrain and keep my prankster side at bay. I decided I wanted to see my wife curtsy, since I had never before seen that.

I called out to my wife, saying, "Come meet the Prince!"

I thought she was going to kill me later. She knew I "got" her, but the joke turned out to be on me, as she eloquently came over and curtsied. You would've thought it was second nature to her!

My wife had really not wanted to go on that trip. I assured her that this was a once-in-a-lifetime experience that should not be missed, and I'd pushed strongly for her to go.

She reluctantly agreed. Later she told me that it was one of the greatest trips of her life, and she thanked me profusely for talking her into going.

If you get an opportunity to do things that are out of the norm, I strongly urge you to try it, within reason of course. Force yourself out of your comfort zone sometimes. It will help you grow as a person, and you will make fond memories to forever take with you.

Hole #19

Ken and Julie

As we settle in at Hole 19, traditionally the golfers' "watering hole," or beverage stop after playing a full round of golf, I will share about a time I was playing golf with Ken Barnes of Naples, Florida. He's a close friend of mine and a partner in a business venture. Ken is someone for whom I have tremendous respect. He is an honest person, a good friend, and has a wonderful heart. Ken has been dealt some very unfair things during both his professional and personal life. He has proven to be a man with a strong resolve.

While we were on the golf course, I asked him about the trip from which he had just returned from Cooper Island in the British Virgin Islands. I knew what the main purpose of this trip was.

Ken had dated a girl named Julie for five years. They had married, spending five additional years together as husband and wife, but also as best friends. I was not privileged to have known Julie, but I have only heard good things about her from everyone who knew her. Ken and Julie had a very special relationship… The kind of relationship all couples dream of having. You can visibly see it in Ken's eyes when he speaks about her.

Julie had been misdiagnosed with colon cancer. Eventually, they discovered she actually had an extremely rare form of appendix cancer. She had been given three months to live. But Ken and Julie refused to accept that. They fought the battle side by side for two-and-a-half years before cancer tragically won out, taking Julie when she was only 42 years old.

Health insurance money ran out before the 2½ -year battle had concluded. The bill-paying responsibility fell on Ken to handle, and he refused to give up at any cost. He began to use and eventually pretty much deplete his life savings.

I won't disclose how much it was, but it was very substantial. Julie and Ken had done some traveling together through their years together and had some wonderful memories, as couples with this kind of magic typically do. Before passing, Julie had asked Ken to spread her ashes in 14 of those places they loved so much.

I asked of Ken how the trip had gone for him. I knew it had to be traumatic for him to gather with mutual friends of his and Julie's, and then return to several of their special places to continue the process of returning with her, for one final time. He told me how he had several of the 14 urns with him and had spread her ashes as she had wished.

He said he then had rented some scuba gear and decided to dive into a cave about 60 feet down off the coast. As he entered the dark cave, he noticed ahead a bright light of sun rays streaming downward through the water. They were coming through an opening above the cave.

As he swam closer to this area of projected light, he felt the current of bluish-green water swirling around him. Glancing around, he noticed beautiful coral, colorful fish, and some seaweed swaying side to side, as though a light summer breeze was blowing it slowly, back and forth.

He'd decided it was a perfect place to lodge the now mostly empty urn that had transported his beautiful Julie one last time to one of their special places. As he carefully secured it in its final resting place, he felt what he described as the hair on his body raising.

He did not think much more about it at the time, but after he surfaced and was on the boat, he learned that the others with him had experienced the same sensation. They all believed that was strange that they all had felt it at the same time.

The sailboat that had taken them all there had an on-deck shower, so Ken decided to rinse the salt water off his body. As he was standing under the water rinsing off, he felt something in the pocket of his swimming trunks.

Knowing that when he had descended below into the water his pocket had been empty, and, of course, being curious, he placed his hand into his pocket to remove this new object. When he opened his fist, he looked in shock at what lay in the palm of his hand. It was a water-carved rock, shaped in the form of a *heart!!*

Ken told me he had never believed much in the paranormal world, but he also said he had no explanation for how that rock, a heart-shaped rock, got in his pocket.

I have had a number of experiences in my life for which I had almost undeniable proof supporting influence from the beyond. That's not what this book is about.

However, next I will share one more golf story that, while it lacks strong evidence, does inspire me with its influence from beyond.

Golf Gimme 19:

A Birthday Gift from "The Beyond"

As stated earlier, when I was a boy, my father had wanted me to play golf. He was an even par-type golfer and loved the game so much.

Though I tried it several times, I just could not see what he saw in the game and had no interest in playing golf. I was busy playing football, basketball, and other more "cool" rural Ohio-type sports. I guess it was good that no one told a kid named Jack Nicklaus, also from Ohio, that golf was not cool! I simply could not see golf in my future. Dad was disappointed, probably more than he let on to me. But he did not force it down my throat.

Dad with John Gehrisch

The Golf Pro Has Heart

After college, I again tried playing golf a few times with Dad. We had many laughs, mostly at my expense. Once I hit a ball high into the air traveling sideways into another fairway.

Dad found it hysterical when my ball found in its new home in the back of someone's "moving" golf cart. Because of my strength and athleticism, I could hit a golf ball pretty far, but I had no idea where it was going to go. I was lucky I did not kill someone those first few times I played.

Once, I thought I would have to carry Dad into the clubhouse on his home course as he tried to recover from laughing after I hit a tee shot that careened off the women's tee marker in front of us. We watched as the ball literally flew back over our heads and out of bound behind the tee.

"I have never seen anyone hit a ball into that cornfield before," Dad said, while he wiped away the tears from laughter. He and the guys playing with us that day certainly found it was funnier than I did. Even I had to laugh a little, as I tried to hide my humiliation.

Now that I have aged, and I look back, it has turned from a youthful embarrassment into a funny lifetime memory with my very best friend… my father. But at that point, I still could not understand the attraction to the game.

Earlier in the book, I mentioned that Phil Porter, one of my then co-workers and now great friend, talked me into trying golf again. Phil was really responsible for my becoming hooked on the game and the wonderful experiences that would follow.

Fortunately, I was able to pay Phil back 40 years later, by arranging for him to play with his lifetime idol and my great friend, Billy Casper. Phil had the time of his life!

If you never met the legend and gentlemen, Billy Casper, before he passed away, that is a shame. Along with his family, he was a gift from God to the world.

A Birthday Gift from "The Beyond"

After I became an adult and had moved out on my own, my father and I lived 1000 miles or more apart. It became special for us to play golf the few times a year we were able to visit the other.

As you probably know, getting a "hole-in-one" is highly unlikely. *Golf Digest* estimated that the odds for the average golfer to be 12,000-to-one. Many golfers and even some current tour professionals have never had a "hole-in-one."

One of the exceptional moments that my Dad and I shared was that I was with my Dad when he made his one-and-only "hole-in-one." Better yet, he was with me when I got my first one! That in itself is extraordinary. Now, add to that the fact that he was with me when I made my first one! I have never met anyone who has had that happen.

As Andy, my own son, grew, he began to want to play golf with Dad and me. He knew about the two very special moments we had shared together. As he improved, he tried so very hard to get a "hole-in-one" when he played with us. He wanted to be a member in our elite club and a part of our father/son legacy and upgrade it to a father/son/grandson legacy.

He would concentrate harder than I ever saw him concentrate. He would come so very close, so many times. But naturally, the odds were severely stacked against him.

Andy's grandfather passed before Andy was able to score an ace with us. They were very close, and Andy was crushed that he had not been able to make a "hole-in-one" happen for his grandfather and father.

One of the many things my father left us was the love for the game, and the special moments and memories that we would continue to share through the years to follow because of it.

Several years after my father had passed on, Andy and I were playing at the Manchester Country Club in New Hampshire. We were on Hole #13, the same hole on which I achieved my first "hole-in-one," while my father was there.

The pin was in a similar position as when I had made my ace. Andy struck the most beautiful shot, just like he had done many times before with his grandfather and me. It travelled directly over the flag landing on the green taking one bounce forward away from the hole. Then it slowly began to draw back towards the hole, getting closer and closer.

Then the magic happened. It slipped over the edge and fell into the cup. Andy and I looked at each other with tears building in our eyes. I could not speak.

Andy then broke the silence with, "Oh, how I wish Gramps was here!"

"He was Andy," I responded. "He was," I assured him again.

We went to the green. We both looked slowly into the hole to verify our eyes had not deceived us. Sure enough, it was lying in the bottom of the cup.

"Looks like *you* are buying, son," I said. "Congratulations!" He had not only accomplished one of the most elusive and desired feats in golf, he had done it with his father!!!

A number of years later I achieved what my father had dreamed for me. I had exited the business world and turned pro, playing on several tours, being paid to play tournaments in other parts of the world, and eventually experiencing the Mini Tours and even some of the Champions Tour.

My father never got to see it when he was alive. But like Andy's "hole-in-one", I like to think he saw it anyway. Maybe he was even a little proud of me.

A Birthday Gift from "The Beyond"

Let's face it. Every son or daughter wants their parents to be proud. And every parent wants their children to be proud of them, too. I guess it is an evolutionary part of life.

I have so wished that my father could have shared in the amazing experiences I lived. If he had only been able to meet many of the wonderful people with whom I played and got to know because of *his* beloved game.

He and I had shared moments together watching many of those golfing stars on TV. Stars he knew of long before I had been able to appreciate the game he so wanted me to love.

Through the following years, I made more "aces." But my son never saw any of them. However, on this week, something amazing was about to happen.

Andy, my first cousin Ron, and I were all going to be in Naples, Florida, at the same time. We had decided to connect for dinner.

I told Ron that Andy and I were going to play and invited him to join us.

He said, "I've only played once with you. I'd love to! I have a friend in town, Jay Tull. Would he be welcome also?"

I said, "Sure! That gives us a foursome."

The next day happened to be Andy's 42nd birthday. I had just turned 64 the day before, and my cousin Ron was 67.

I now believe that my Dad and his sister (Ron's mother) were there watching us from above on that day. In life, when Dad and his sister got together, no one ever knew what to expect. In so many ways, they were both two of the most amazing people I have ever known.

As we played the second hole, I recalled to Ron, Jay, and Andy, the only eulogy I ever really remembered. It was the one Ron had given at his mother's funeral. I remembered being in awe that he could even speak in that situation, as I knew how close he had been with his mother.

Silence had overtaken the room when he entered, as everyone watched him in wonder. He had walked to the front and peered into the coffin where she was laid peacefully. You could hear a pin drop.

It was the last time any of us would see her for a long time. Ron had stood for several moments, gazing at her silent face. He then walked to the podium and began to speak.

"As I stood looking at mother," he started, "would anyone here doubt me, if I told you she looked up at me, and winked?"

No one would have! She had come from the same stock my Great Grandparents, Grandparents, and father. The same playful stock from which most of us in the room had come. It would not have surprised any of us at all!

He actually brought a moment of levity to a very hurting group. I will never forget his grace and composure. I know how proud his mother was at that moment. I know how proud of him we all were!

Anyway, back to the golf course. We all smiled as we talked and proceeded down the fairway together. Imagine, many years after her passing, here on this golf course she was right there with us again. We all knew it.

Many times, I can feel my father with me as I have walked fairways, too. I can hear him as the leaves blow and the bird's chirp, just as I did when we played so many years ago. I miss those days more than I can ever explain. It makes me cherish, even more, these moments now with my own son.

A Birthday Gift from "The Beyond"

Maybe my father and aunt were pleased that we were continuing the family bonds they had displayed to us during their lives. After all, no one was ever closer than my father and the sister he adored! It is so much harder now for those of us that remain, as the distance between us makes it such a challenge. No one ever took those two siblings for granted or knew what to expect from them.

I believe those two pranksters decided to make something special happen this day. Something more remarkable than anyone could ever even have imagined writing in a novel.

The course was new to Ron, Jay, and me. The weather was perfect. Panthers Run was in wonderful condition. We were enjoying a perfect day, jabbing each other as we walked up on the 7th tee. It was a short par three with a front left pin placement, playing about 135 yards, based on the current wind condition.

I had the honors as I had just made a birdie on the previous hole. I pulled my 9-iron and teed up the ball. I looked down at my Titleist resting on the tee for a moment. It was sitting higher than I would normally play it. This was not supposed to be a serious round of golf, so I justified hitting it as it sat, rather than stooping over and re-teeing it correctly.

I took my stance and made what felt like a tour quality swing… the kind I only occasionally accomplish now.

Looking up after making contact, I watched the ball flying straight at the hole. Ping had just sent me new I15 clubs, and I wasn't even sure if the yardage was correct for my new club. I watched the ball continue toward the target and drop on the green. It took a hop towards the hole and disappeared from my sight.

As it was a raised tee box, above the cart path where the others stood, I was in the highest vantage point to see the pin, as I stood between the tee markers. I thought the ball might have gone in, but I wasn't sure because there was a possibility the hump was hiding the ball. I turned and noticed Andy had grabbed the yardage laser and was looking through the binocular section from the cart.

"Dad," he said, "I don't see the ball."

I said, "I think it might have gone in."

No one was sure, so no premature celebrations took place.

The others hit their shots, and we ventured up to the green. There was no ball to be seen from the cart path.

Andy and I remained seated in the cart, as we saw that Jay had left his cart and was walking briskly up to the green. He paused slightly short of the hole and began to sneak up on the hole. Slowly he peered over the edge of the cup.

Why do we always sneak up on the hole to check if a ball is "in" for holes-in-one? LOL

"It's in!" he exclaimed.

I looked at Andy, still sitting to my right. His hand went up and he gave me a "High-Five."

I stood up out of the cart, and I turned towards the hole and saw Ron approaching with his hand extended in congratulations. Jay also ran over and gave me the ball and shook my hand.

I then turned back towards Andy, standing there now, and received a second "High-Five" from him. It was only then that I realized I had once more closed the loop between father and son.

I had now scored a *"hole-in-one"* with *my* son, who had already done it with me, just as my father and I had done so many years before. Without realizing it, the task had been mine all these years. But now, at last, it was completed two generations in a row.

I wonder if it has ever been done before. I sincerely doubt it.

But what added to the moment was the fact that my father had only one sibling. And his sister's only son, my only male cousin from either side, was with us, too!!! Someone I had played golf with only one other time in 64 years!!

And, incredibly, it had happened on my son's birthday!

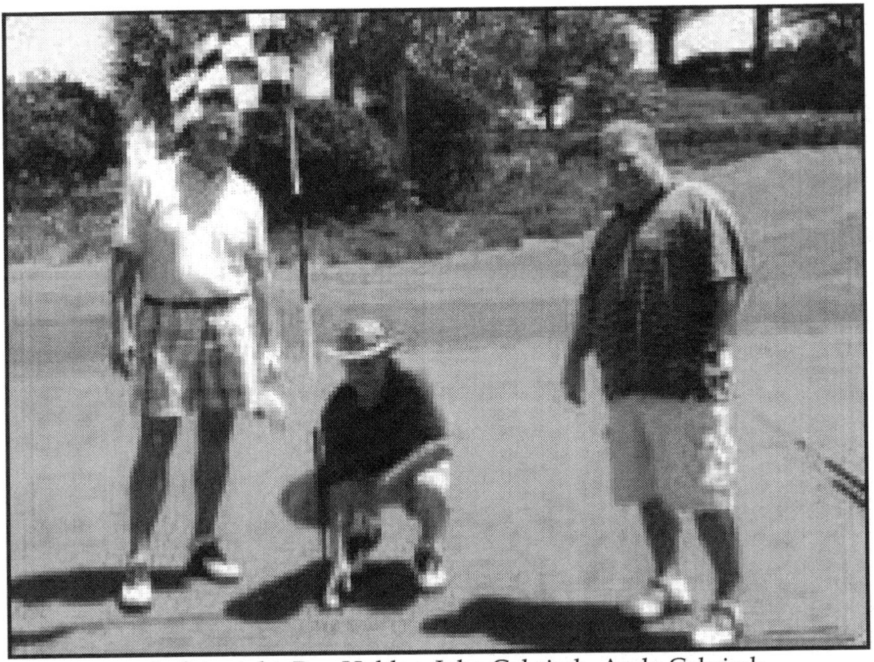

Left to right: Ron Holden, John Gehrisch, Andy Gehrisch

What a day!

Just try and tell any of us there that day that Dad and my Aunt were not present too!! You'd never get us to buy it! In fact, I could not help wondering who else from the family was watching.

I sat at my son's home later that night reflecting on the day. While playing the first 5 holes that day I had been working on trying to recover some of the distance I had lost through the last 10 years because of cancer, surgeries, and an increase in age.

I had accomplished my swing changes fairly well on the range, but had struggled on taking it to the course during the first 5 holes. I decided to go back to my normal swing on the 6th tee to better enjoy the day, and had been rewarded with a birdie.

The hole-in-one on #7 had followed, and then a birdies on #8 and #9. I finished the day with 5 birdies and 2 eagles, something I rarely do anymore.

It occurred to me that had I *not* been experimenting early in the round and just played my normal golf that entire day, only making par on the first five holes, I might have shot my age for the first time. That would have been another rarity that my son and cousin could have shared.

No matter what, I am grateful for the best ever birthday gift that my son and I received that day. "A birthday gift" that had been sent to us, "from The Beyond!!"

Driving Home

Only You Can Prevent Forest Fires

"The key to a successful relationship is to clear your internet history."
-- Unknown

I now refer to Smokey the Bear's famous quote, *"Only You Can Prevent Forest Fires."* I adapted it a little to, *"Only You Can Chose a Happy, Loving, Long-Term Relationship!"*

If you are not in a relationship, you can be smarter now and more selective in the choice of your mate. On that note, consider the following list of 100 Things You Should Know About Your Potential Mate. Not that you will sit and do an interview with your date, unless you want them to think you are off-balance. However, in the course of normal conversation, do be sure to take into consideration how compatible this person is with you.

In typical conversation you will learn the answers to most of these questions. Some, however, need to be addressed directly.

100 Things You Should Know About Your Potential Mate

1. How good of a communicator are they?
2. Are they a sociable person or an introvert?
3. Have they ever been arrested, or in jail or prison?
4. Are there any emotions they have trouble controlling?
5. What kind of baggage do they bring with them?
6. Have they ever had a restraining order placed against them by anyone?
7. Are they mentally and physically available, i.e. Single? Divorced? Widowed?
8. What kind of relationship do they have with their ex?
9. Do they already have children? If so, the number, their sex, their ages?
10. What are the custody arrangements?

11. If they already have children, how much time do they spend with them?
12. Why did their past relationship end? How long did it last?
13. Do you both agree about having or not having children? If yes, how many?
14. Have they ever been to counseling either with or without their partner?
15. What is their longest committed relationship?
16. Do they believe in being monogamous?
17. Have they ever cheated in a committed relationship?
18. Have they ever slept with anyone who tested positive for a sexual disease?
19. Have they ever had to be treated for venereal disease?
20. Do they use protection, and, if so, at what point in a relationship do they stop?
21. Are they comfortable talking about sex?
22. Do they have anything they need to work on in order to build a good relationship with you?
23. Do they like spending time with children?
24. What kind of activities have they done with children, i.e. coaching, mentoring, hobbies?
25. If you have children together, will both people be expected to work outside the home?
26. What do they value most about the opposite sex?
27. What is their level of education and how important is that to you?
28. Are they religious? Do they go to church? If so, how often and what type?
29. Do you like the way they dress?
30. Do they smoke?
31. Do they drink alcohol? How often do they drink? Do they enjoy getting drunk?
32. Do they do any drugs?
33. What kind of music do they enjoy?
34. Are they employed, and, if so, for how long?
35. Do they set goals? If so what are their plans for the future?
36. Is their personality to be a workaholic? A perfectionist? An intellect? An athlete?
37. Do they have their life under control?

38. What would they change about their life if they could? Do they have a plan to do it?
39. What do they feel is there most troubling failure? What would they have done differently?
40. Are they good about managing money?
41. Are they financially secure?
42. Do you agree on philosophies regarding spending or saving money?
43. How do your philosophies coincide regarding borrowing money?
44. Do they own their own home, or live in an apartment? How do they see the future on this?
45. If you decide to live together or get married, in whose place will you live?
46. Who will do the housework? One of you or both of you?
47. How does their attitude regarding materialistic possessions match yours?
48. How much free time do they have now?
49. What did they do in their free time to relax?
50. Do they do any volunteering?
51. What do they enjoy spending time doing with the opposite sex?
52. Do they have a hobby?
53. Do they enjoy reading, if so what kind of material?
54. Have they done any kind of self-improvement programs? For what reason?
55. What is their decision-making process? Does it differ if they have a partner?
56. Do they play sports? If so what kind and how often?
57. Do they enjoy watching sports on TV, or attending games?
58. What kind of TV programs do they enjoyed besides sports?
59. Do they belong to any singles groups or dating sites?
60. If so, at what point in the relationship are they willing to give those up?
61. Are they interested in companionship only, or a long-term relationship?
62. What type of vacations do they like?
63. Do they prefer going on vacations alone or with a partner?
64. Are they adventuresome and enjoy trying new things?

65. Are staying healthy and eating properly important to them?
66. Are they a certain type of eater? i.e. Vegetarian? Vegan?
67. What kind of foods or restaurants do they enjoy?
68. How often do they like to eat out?
69. Do they cook?
70. Do they keep up with current events?
71. How strong are their political views, if any? Do your philosophies blend, if that is important to you?
72. Do they like animals?
73. Do they have any pets?
74. Are you allergic to any of the pets they have?
75. Are they allergic to any of your pets?
76. What kind a sense of humor do they have? Does it match yours?
77. Are they a leader or follower, and how does that match your personality?
78. What type of personalities do or did their parents have?
79. What was their childhood like growing up?
80. What kind of friends did they associate with growing up?
81. What kind of relationship did they have with their parents growing up?
82. What kind of relationship do they have with their parents now?
83. Which parent was more influential as they grew up?
84. Who are they closer to now, their mother or their father?
85. What type of friends do they prefer?
86. How often do they spend time with friends, and how do they describe them?
87. What have they enjoyed doing with their friends most of the time?
88. Will their time with their friends interfere with a relationship with you?
89. If you made a surprise visit, what would their apartment look like? Messy? Organized? How does that match with your style of living?
90. What kind of personality do they have? Are they a Giver? Or Taker?
91. Are they an affectionate person? How important is that to you?

92. What percentage of the time are they a positive person versus negative?
93. How do they feel about and the handle arguments? Does this feel normal and acceptable to you?
94. How do you both feel about showing affection in public?
95. Are they a sensual or sexual person? How does that blend with you?
96. How romantic are they? How does that match with what you want?
97. Are they a caring and sensitive person?
98. Do they show empathy towards others, or are they more self-centered?
99. What is your take on their integrity and honesty?
100. What is their age? Is age only a number to you, or does it matter?

If you are already in a relationship that has not hit serious problems yet, but does not match the JAG formula perfectly, you and your mate *can* be on the lookout for potential problems and identify them. Those 100 question areas can still be very helpful in your discussions.

In fact, keep this book handy and refer back to it whenever you need a refresher or more and better tools.

It helps us when we gain an understanding of why things are happening and how to solve them.

If you are in a deeply troubled relationship, you may desire to make an attempt to salvage it. It is my belief that knowing what works for those who *are* happy will give *you* the tools you need to reach the goal of becoming more like them.

We cannot become someone we are not. But when we understand what and why things are happening, and where we need to be for things to work better, then we may have a possible way to salvage things enough to save the marriage.

You may not have perfect harmony. Still, many people do not want to divorce, whether because of religion, the children, or other personal beliefs. Regardless, why not try to make things more palatable and happy?

If you are like me when I wrote this, already divorced and not wanting to make another mistake, then this should give you the tools to be smarter, should you get into another relationship. Let's face it, most of us are pretty much designed to not want to be alone.

Let's have our future full. I wish you a very ***Happy, Loving, Long-Term Relationship!***

Remember to share your ideas for Mystery Dates and Romantic Rendezvous with your significant other on our website:

www.GolfProHasHeart.com

Bonus Golf Gimme:

Pebble Beach Gag

I played the Pebble Beach Invitational Golf Tournament for a number of years. One year, I was teamed up with an amateur by the name of Jeff Houston. He asked me if I had ever experienced a Chef's Table. I told him I had not.

Jeff informed me that he and his wife, Janine, planned to try one at an exclusive local resort. He invited my wife and me to go with them. Putting aside the fact that this was one of the most expensive dinners I've ever had, it was quite an experience. The chef came to our table with each of the eight courses.

He explained the preparation and the wine pairing. The table was actually located in the kitchen, so we could observe the operations. Sometimes the Chef's Tables are not in the kitchen itself, so this was a treat.

After dinner we walked upstairs, and the girls mentioned they needed to use the restroom. So, Jeff and I also went to the restroom. Jeff went to the urinal, and I went into one of the stalls. I ripped off about 6 feet of toilet paper, tucked one end in the back of my shoe, and the other end in my belt. I walked quickly to open the door before Jeff got there. Holding the door open for him with my back to the door, he could not see the toilet paper.

I began to walk with him, but stayed about one-half step behind, as I dropped the toilet paper end that was in my pants. Now, trailing behind me, was a 6-foot trail of toilet paper, flipping up into the air with each step I took.

As we walked into the lobby the girls were waiting and watching for us. They spotted us coming and began to laugh hysterically.

Jeff said, "What are the girls laughing at?" He looked around and spotted the toilet paper following me. "OH, GARRISH!" (That's the way my name is pronounced.)

When we reached the girls, no one asked me to remove the toilet paper, so we continued to walk through the lobby toward the front door. The girls behind the reservation desk began to lose it in laughter. The people waiting to check in turned around to see what they were laughing at. As they spotted me and my toilet paper tail, they began to laugh also.

Now the entire lobby was watching and laughing as we walked. Naturally, we acted like we didn't know what was going on.

As we exited the front door and began down the steps towards the valet, he was already waiting with our car and noticed the toilet paper following me.

As the paper took the shape of each and every step behind me, he began to laugh hysterically. Jeff and I open the doors for the ladies on the passenger side, and they entered the car. We then walked around to the driver's side. The valet handed me the keys as I handed him his gratuity.

He said to me, "Thank you so much for adding some levity here. Everyone is usually so stuffy. It's great to see people laughing and having a good time."

I responded, "Hey! That is what life *should* be all about. Life is too short not to have fun."

I wish you fun in your life, like the Golf Pro Who Has Heart, and, of course, a *Happy, Loving, Long-Term Relationship*.

About the Author

Not every electrical engineer can parlay a successful sales and marketing career into the professional golf circuit. But John A. Gehrisch is far from typical.

Not one to remain idle, he is a co-partner in a commercial real estate development and management company. Also, President of BBJM Golf Ventures, the exclusive golf memorabilia producer since 2003, John has enjoyed golf since he got out of college. It was his Dad who dreamed of John becoming a tour golf professional.

That was after founding and running a successful wire and cable insulating company, PMC Corporation, which, prior to its sale, produced enough wire in one year to wrap around the world 13 times. It's no wonder that financial guru Warren Buffet chose to purchase PMC Corporation.

This enabled Gehrisch to direct successful turnarounds for struggling companies. He was honored to serve on the New Hampshire Governors Round Table and the U.S. Presidential Round Table.

Golf remained his passion. As soon as he turned pro in 1999, he started playing on the mini tours, finishing second several times prior to winning his first event on the Western States Tour in early 2000. He has played on and off on the Senior PGA Tour (now the Champions Tour) and been paid to compete in international professional tournaments as far away as the Azores and Morocco.